My Winds of Change

Wilhelm Verwoerd

RAVAN PRESS

Published by Ravan Press, 1997
PO Box 145 Randburg 2125 South Africa

© Wilhelm Verwoerd 1997

All rights reserved. No part of this publication may be reproduced, stored in a retrieval system, or transmitted in any form or by any means, electronic, mechanical, photocopying, or otherwise, without the prior permission of the copyright owner.

Cover design: Centre Court Studio
Typesetting: Niamb Simons

English edition by Herman Fourie

ISBN 0 86975 513 7

Printed and bound by
National Book Printers, Drukkery Street, Goodwood, Western Cape

Foreword

The ANC offers a political home to all South Africans. But the journey into its ranks can sometimes be a difficult one. Our social backgrounds and the attitudes of communities to which we belong combine with the circumstances of the times to put a great variety of challenges in the path of political choice and decision. This was especially so during the struggle for liberation and in the early years of our transition, when such decisions could be a matter of life and death, or bring ostracism and the loss of community.

Seldom can these factors have combined to demand an inner struggle of such intensity as that traced in the pages of this book.

Family ties; the cultural web woven by education and religion; bonds of ethnicity distorted precisely to fashion the Afrikaner community into a monolith without individual choice, and to divide the Afrikaner from the majority of fellow South Africans – all these conspired to confront the young Wilhelm Verwoerd with an almost impossible choice.

The terms in which he wrestled with his inherited circumstances may well feel unfamiliar to most South Africans. And yet through the detail they will discern the effort we all have to make to free ourselves from the conceptions of our divided past. All of us will recognise the challenge of embracing the liberation that comes with forsaking the thinking that pits one community against another; the liberation that comes with seeking our future within a larger society whose unity depends on the flourishing of its rich diversity.

Publishing the record of this very Afrikaans struggle in English should help more people understand something of the experience of brave compatriots "in the belly of the beast" as they set about becoming part of a new South Africa.

We can all be thankful that freedom has taken the danger out of political choice. But the building of a non-racial, non-sexist and democratic society has just begun. It will continue to confront each and every person with choices that will not always be easy. It is a protracted process which demands the active participation of every section of society.

May this record of personal courage inspire us all to join hands with one another in building a nation in which each and every individual and community feels at home.

Mandela

NELSON MANDELA
Republic of South Africa
June 1997

Contents

Foreword

List of illustrations   between pages 88 and 89

1. Introduction: My Winds of Change   1
2. From Soldier for Jesus to a Tree in the Wind   7
3. From white Afrikaner to "pigment-poor" "afrika-ner"   67
4. From grandson to "prodigal son"   107
5. From "my girlfriend and I" to "Melanie's husband"   143
6. Conclusion: A Commitment to Continuing Conversions   164

    Select Bibliography   172

    Acknowledgements   176

*If you bring forth what is in you, what you bring forth will save you;
If you do not bring forth what is in you, what you do not bring forth will destroy you.*

Jesus Christ, Gospel of St Thomas

The task is not finished. South Africa is not yet a home for all her sons and daughters ... There remains before us the building of a new land, a home for men who are black, white, brown, from the ruins of the old narrow groups, a synthesis of the rich cultural strains which we have inherited. There remains to be achieved our integration with the rest of our continent. Somewhere ahead there beckons a civilisation, a culture, which will take its place in the parade of God's history beside other great human syntheses, Chinese, Egyptian, Jewish, European. It will not necessarily be all black; but it will be African.

More than other continents, perhaps, and as much as any other nation of this continent, we need the ways of peace, the ways of industry, the ways of concord.

Albert Luthuli, Let My People Go, *1962*

Chapter 1

Introduction

"Viva Verwoerd!" people were shouting in the audience, in between all the other calls: "One President, one Mandela!", "Viva ANC, Viva!". It moved me deeply. "Verwoerd in tears over cheers" said a newspaper headline the next day.

The time was eight o'clock on 13 May 1993 and I was sitting on the stage at the Parow Civic Centre. Outside, the posters in green, gold and black bore the speakers' names: NIEHAUS, BOESAK and VERWOERD – ANC MEETING. The hall was packed to capacity and a riot of noise and colour – election posters, balloons, flowers; there was even an Afrikaans copy of Nkosi Sikelel'iAfrika on each chair. Outside the hall the police and peace monitors had their work cut out to separate African National Congress supporters and the far-right Afrikaner Weerstandsbeweging (AWB).

I had been tense and nervous about addressing a meeting in this conservative, white, Afrikaans part of Cape Town. Chris Hani[1] had been gunned down shortly before; there had been warnings that the AWB was planning to arrive in large numbers to break up the meeting in their anger about this new "traitor" siding with a "bunch of black communists and terrorists".

When it was my turn to speak I struggled to get my first words past the lump in my throat: "Ladies and gentlemen, friends, opponents and ... comrades!"

"Comrades"? I had agonised about using this word, so laden with negative associations in the minds of especially Afrikaners. Yet it is a crucial term, reflecting the tragic "success" of Apartheid, but also containing a lot of promise for the future. I had used the word as a young Voortrekker (Afrikaner Boy Scout) in the 1970s, when we sang the German hiking song "Kamerad, Kamerad" on our out-

---

[1] Very popular former commander of the ANC's military wing, leader of the SACP, tragically assassinated in April 1993 by white rightwingers.

ings. While we sang our carefree songs many less fortunate young South Africans were being killed in the townships or were fleeing the country to join their comrades in the struggle against Apartheid. Now, a few years later, I was standing on an ANC platform together with some of these comrades.

My speech dealt with this central question: *Was it possible to be liberated from Apartheid, so deeply rooted in the hearts and minds of so many of us? Was it possible to find common ground between Voortrekker "kamerade" and ANC comrades, while so many South Africans continued to live in separated worlds?*

I tried briefly to give a positive answer to this question, without being too idealistic and ended my speech with these words:

"I still find it awkward to say 'comrade', especially using the Afrikaans version 'kameraad'. I am still getting used to toyi-toyi. I still have much to unlearn and much to learn. But the bottom line is: it is exciting and liberating to join in the cameraderie of, let's call it our "Comrades Marathon" towards a new South Africa free from oppression in our homes, in our factories and mines, in our politics!

"I had wondered whether I should end with a 'Viva ANC', but for the time being I will end with this invitation to especially the more timid, paler ones of us here tonight – Come, run with us!"

So ended my first, liberating appearance on an ANC stage. It drew out a barrage of questions from all manner of people: "How could you, a grandson of the Architect of Apartheid, join the ANC?", "How could an Afrikaner turn his back on his people to join a communist alliance?", "How could you do that to your parents?", "Was it your own decision or did your wife Melanie influence you?", "Did you do it as penance for the Verwoerds' involvement in Apartheid?", "What is a Christian like you doing in a violent, communist organisation?" and "Why did you only join in 1992?" (as if to say "Where were you when we were sitting in jail?").

My response to these pressing questions had to wait until after 27 April 1994. The run-up to our first truly democratic election did not leave much room for reflection. This liberating participation in an election victory and the honeymoon months after the (relatively) peaceful "small miracle" made it difficult to remember the long journey to a Saturday morning in May 1992, when, at last, I signed my name (and surname) on an ANC membership application form. At home the noisy growing pains of two small children made it even more tempting to suppress the many questioning voices following that meeting in Parow. However, I could still hear my father's silence. His suspension of questioning – and our relationship – prompted me to start writing, trying to explain why a particularly crunching choice was made.

Many hours spent in heated arguments and fruitless debate taught me that another appeal to reason was doomed to fail. One alternative was to try and tell "my story" as honestly and humbly as possible. Diaries, various other writings and letters – especially those I wrote to Melanie while I studied in Holland and England – helped me to recount some of the events leading up to May 1992. More importantly, these writings – often scribbled late at night and in a prayerful, searching spirit – enabled me to remember the less visible events, the deep changes in different parts of myself, which made a raised Viva fist on an ANC stage possible.

This retelling and reliving of the moral and existential struggle with my own "traitor's heart" and the "sins of the fathers" – in the (Dutch Reformed) Church, in the Afrikaner "volk", in my family, at home – soon took on a bigger life of its own, beyond a private attempt to rebuild the relationship with my father. I became much more aware of the struggles of many white, mainly Afrikaans-speaking students at Stellenbosch University, to find a home in post-Apartheid, affirmative action South Africa. I became more frustrated with the political correctness and denials of responsibility for Apartheid amongst many privileged white South Africans. I became more concerned about often suppressed feelings of fear, of guilt and shame, lurking behind their anger against the ANC – "if you do not bring forth what is in you, what you do not bring forth will destroy you".

I, therefore, continued to attempt answering those questions, focusing less on ANC policies and practices and more on the changes underlying my choice to join a liberation movement which, allegedly, wants to "enslave the Afrikaner". I did this with the hope that such an account of a process of personal "reconstruction and development", of the gradual transformation of debilitating guilt feelings into a more creative acceptance of responsibility, of a liberating reconciliation between the various parts of myself, would contribute to reconciliation ... inside and outside my family.

The first written attempt to "bring forth what is in me" was completed by the end of 1994. My father was not very impressed with his Christmas present. I underestimated the depth of his feelings about that "fist" (and his father). By October 1995 the Afrikaans manuscript was revised and accepted for publication. Now it is February 1997 and I have the opportunity to tell these stories in English.

Sometimes I wonder whether I should make use of this opportunity, given the different backgrounds and experiences of non-Afrikaans-speaking readers. Quite a few things have also changed. It is, for example, more difficult to be an ANC member (especially in a Western Cape province still dominated by the NP). The ANC-led government's honeymoon is over and we can no longer blame the NP or Apartheid for most things. Making democracy work and implementing the RDP (together with GEAR) is indeed proving to be a "comrades marathon" – but an unexpectedly difficult, slow and uphill one. Everybody is now (very) worried about crime. Trade union leaders are investing on the stock exchange. Unemployment has increased. On a personal level, I am no longer teaching Political Philosophy and Applied Ethics (on the 6th floor of a BJ Vorster building), but trying to practise what I've "preached", as a researcher within the Truth and Reconciliation Commission. We've moved from "Paradise Valley", Stellenbosch, to a new home in the windswept shadow of Devil's Peak, Cape Town, to survive as a family with a MP for a mother (and partner).

However, some things have not changed. Not many of my paler fellow South Africans have accepted the invitation to participate in the marathon, at least not as "comrades". Many people still find it painful and confusing to change, especially those who have much to say sorry for. A central question remains: *Is it possible to be liberated from Apartheid, so deeply rooted in the hearts and minds of so many of us? Is it possible to find common ground between Voortrekker "kamerade" and ANC comrades (amongst others), while so many South Africans continue to live in separated worlds?* After almost five years the separation from my father continues, I am still not welcome in his house.

Thus I am continuously reminded that reconciliation is not a quick fix. And my current participation in a painfilled process to "bring forth" the dark sides in our pasts strengthens my conviction that being "saved" from destructive conflicts, especially between beneficiaries and the disadvantaged, does not come cheaply. The links between truth and reconciliation cannot be taken for granted.

After two-and-a-half years we have a disturbingly long way to go to deliver on the election promise of a million new houses by 1999. Working within the TRC is reminding me, however, that there might be an even more difficult unfinished task. For South Africa is indeed "not yet **a home** for all her sons and daughters ... there remains before us the building of a new land, a home for men [sic] who are black, white, brown, from the ruins of the old narrow groups" (Luthuli) (my emphasis).

Inspired by this vision and motivated by my experience that reconciliation begins at home – with coming home to oneself – I want to take the risk of sharing some of my stories with other people who probably are also buffeted by the "winds of change" in a new South Africa. Stories about a continuing journey of coming (and staying) home by a particular thirtysomething, white, male, heterosexual, middle-class, urbanised, Christian, Afrikaans-speaking, philosopher, Verwoerd.

It is, of course, not so easy to divide this kind of journey into four different chronicles. I am doing it on purpose: to emphasise, to celebrate some of the many dimensions of someone's personal identity, in a country where reductionist racial and ethnic categories – Luthuli's "narrow groups" – are still deeply entrenched.

I am certain that most people will be more interested in the surname "Verwoerd" than the name "Wilhelm" which was written on that application form. My membership of the Verwoerd family was indeed an important contributing factor to a rather difficult choice. However, there were also a number of other, even more important reasons. To write a single chronicle about why a grandson of THE Architect of Apartheid joined the ANC would be to tear a single chapter from a book and imagine that it could tell the whole story.

Before looking at my "Verwoerdness", I, therefore, want to describe my own "Little Trek" away from a proud and arrogant White Afrikanership (in a note to me at Oxford in 1990 Sir Laurens van der Post had written: "Your letter provides further evidence of the Afrikaners' Great Trek through the world within"). But first I want to recount the very important role played by my particular Christian pilgrimage, starting with the self-confident missionary zeal of a schoolboy "Soldier for Jesus", advancing via disillusioned political "atheism" to the cautious, unpredictable spirituality of a "tree in the wind" (with a green, yellow and black flag entwined in one of its branches).

The last but not least part of my journey towards and beyond a crucial choice deals with my relationship with my wife, Melanie. Among other things it is an account of my journey from a somewhat theoretical non-sexism to a more practical feminism. In it I pay tribute to her role as indispensable midwife in that laborious process.

In the concluding section I shall try to draw together these different strands in a more explicit reflection on the process of deep change or conversion that I describe in these stories. I shall also attempt to integrate this series of often unplanned (and unwanted) rebirths with the current phase of my journey. A journey which makes me look with new eyes to what Jung said towards the end of his life:

"In my pilgrim's progress I had to climb down a thousand ladders to reach out a hand of friendship to this little 'clot' of earth that I am."

Cape Town
15 February 1997

Chapter 2

From Soldier for Jesus to a Tree in the Wind

Happy are those, I hear You say,
who are pure of heart,
because they will see God.
Do you mean those who are afraid
who keep themselves aloof from politics and business?
When I look at You, I see
You working, living and loving
in the midst of this filthy world.
Perhaps the heart will only be pure
when hands are no longer afraid
of illness and human suffering.
             Jörg Zink, Path to Prayer

I was born on 21 February 1964 in the Moedersbond Hospital, Pretoria – the same hospital where Melanie was to see the first light of day three years later. My first birth happened in the time when the dark, long years of Mandela and others on Robben Island were just starting.

I was "born again" on Sunday night, 12 June 1977, almost a year after the death of Hector Petersen and many other young people in Soweto.

My rebirth is described on page 273 of my New Testament, my first grown-up Bible, inscribed as a gift from "Mom and Dad" on my eighth birthday:

"So then because thou art lukewarm, and neither cold nor hot, I will spue thee out of my mouth.

"Because thou sayest, I am rich, and increased with goods, and have need of nothing; and knowest not that thou art wretched, and miserable, and poor, and blind, and naked.

"Behold, I stand at the door, and knock: if any man hear my voice, and open the door, I will come in to him, and will sup with him, and he with me." – Revelation 3:16-17, 20.

Under these verses there is a remark in pencil, "Dominee Ockie preaches wonderfully". Next to it: "12 June 1977, 21h00. I, Dreyer, Hattie and Faffas form the 'SfJ'." These notes are confirmed by an entry in my standard 6A1 "English Diary" (in my own version of English):

"Tonight I heard a wonderful preech by ds. Ockie Raubenheimer. Four of my friends and I decided to form a Christian group which give Bibles and parts of bibles to coloured people, Bantoes and whites."

I remember that there was an unsuccessful attempt by the Devil (?) to distract us that evening, in the shape of a scratching fleabag of a dog venturing into the Union Park Congregation Centre that cold winter's evening in search of warmth.

On reflection I think the "Angel of Light" and a few of his friends did not need a dog to stunt my spiritual growth – my own religiosity sufficed for that. My enthusiasm for handing out Bibles (and "parts of bibles") to "coloured people, Bantoes and whites" did not leave me much time to worry about the fate of Hector Petersen's family and friends. My intense desire for a pure heart kept me away from the "filth of the world's business" (Zink) – a world filled with the structural violence of colonialism, poverty and Apartheid, of riots in Soweto, the "armed struggle", freedom fighters and Viva Mandelas. My strenuous attempts to discern God's shining visage helped to blind me to all that. It was only to be several years after my rebirth that I would begin to see the "Angel of Light" haunting the footsteps of Christian Nationalists and Verwoerdian "Separate Developmentalists" like a faithful hound.

But I do not want to anticipate this tale. Shortly after that fateful Sunday evening in 1977 I dreamt that my school principal summoned me and a few close friends over the intercom: "Would the following Soldiers for Jesus please come to my office at once: Wilhelm Verwoerd, Dreyer Lötter, Francois Smit, Gabriël Kroes". I cannot remember what he had to say, possibly because my previous visit to him had been marked by two firm whacks by cane on the bottom: if one neglected to lift one's behind from the seat when greeting a teacher, the offending part of the anatomy had to pay the penalty.

What the dream confirmed was that our group of Christians had gained both a name and a slogan ("Be not overcome of evil, but overcome evil with good." Romans 12:21) and also that we were fired with the desire to put our ideals into action.

The next few years we worked hard to avoid being "spat out" at the Last Judgement. The Devil's work for idle hands lay in the attic, gathering dust on Sunday afternoons, while we were out conducting Bible study classes and praying, or otherwise holding Sunday school for the "coloured people" on nearby farms, "teaching them how to pray". To counteract any sign of idleness or lukewarmth we had ordered dozens of Bible extracts and tracts from religious organisations on which "Soldiers for Jesus, Telephone 71427/6041/ ..." had to be handwritten. During the week these were handed out to (white) pupils at school, or in town, to coloured people, a few "whities" and even a "Bantu" or two – at that stage influx control was still working well in the "Coloured preference area" of the Western Cape.

We did not only pray, read the Bible and hand out tracts: the English diaries of my high school years testify to an awareness that the "fight for Jesus" was not restricted to "spirits in the air" (Eph.6); school military cadet training and "Youth Preparedness" periods served to prepare us for the "Total Onslaught".

11-18 August 1978
Friday – and at one o'clock a few of us left in Bedford trucks from the school to Radio East Cape where our Cadettes would spend the week end under the Army's leadership ... We drilled until about five o'clock and afterwards had to get our places ready in the tents. In the evening we got two lectures on Communism and radios. The one on Communism was full of very interesting facts, but the Captain who talked had a very boring voice so I almost fell asleep ...

Friday 29 June 1979
We were asked today in class to write down our opinions about war ... I don't think there are very much to say in favour of wars because it mostly destroy people's lives and their belongings ...

One day we will all have to defend our border against numerous attacks from the terrorists, who are getting better and better trained, especially in the last few months, by the East Germans. So far we've lived safe and secure, far from any war and its fearful results. Few of us ever saw a body mutelated or bullit-ridden, but I think we ought to start realising that war is a reality and that we must prepare ourselves physically and much more important, spiritually, because that's where the only answer lies ..."

By standards nine and ten the spiritual preparation of our little band of Soldiers for Jesus had started cooling down. We had made the mistake of involving some of our other friends as well, and they included girls. Before long the religious tracts started gathering dust in the bottom of my cupboard.

This did not immediately mean the end of our "good fight": in February 1982 I enrolled for a BA in Theology at Stellenbosch University, the so-called BA Admission. A sports injury had not only shattered my dreams of becoming a Springbok athlete, but had also kept me from performing my military service straight after school, as my two elder brothers had done.

This meant that instead of doing two years of square-bashing and waging war against the "enemy" outside our borders, I could begin training in the neverending battle against THE enemy, Satan, and the evil lurking in the hearts of all of us.

Three years of Greek, Hebrew, psychology, philosophy and Bible and theological studies would gain me admission to four years of study for the ministry at the famous Stellenbosch Seminary of the (white) Dutch Reformed Church, a faculty irreverently known among students as the "Angel Factory".

As it turned out, I was never admitted, although I was well on the way to becoming an "angel" of the purest variety. Despite three years of regular holiday missionary work, which involved singing and preaching trips through rural Swaziland and the plantations of the Eastern Transvaal (now Mpumalanga), Christian Students' Union beach ministry work at Strandfontein (on the West Coast), fundraising trips for the Admissiebond (theological students' union) bursary scheme, of which I had been elected chairman for 1984, hours of copying and photostating minutes as secretary of the Students' Church Youth Action Association, and mostly fruitless attempts at improving the spiritual welfare of "the boys" of Wilgenhof, the notorious Stellenbosch men's residence, I did not proceed to the Seminary.

Luckily some people (or was it someone?) put an end to my long-term career goals. The next four years I spent away from Stellenbosch and the "Angel Factory", and those years did, as I now know, much to help along the progress of this particular pilgrim, especially on my path towards public political involvement. Perhaps my hands were dirtier than they would have been otherwise, but my heart was somewhat purer ...

After completing a BA I wanted to further my studies in what was then a particular interest of mine, psychology. In particular, I was drawn to pastoral psychology, a discipline which combined Christian and psychological counselling, concentrating on practical guidance for people with problems, especially in their marriages. As it was, the lecturer who was due to teach me unexpectedly left the university, and I decided on an honours degree in philosophy for the 1985 academic year instead.

In 1986 I went on to a master's degree, on the theme of suffering and finding a lifestyle which allowed one to make sense out of it. I started a dissertation titled "Humour and Suffering".

These choices, to the extent that they were not due to circumstances beyond my control, also reflect the fact that my first few university years, like my last school years, were not only times of aggressive, "evangelical" Christian activism, but also times when I felt tepid, even frigid amid all the heat. This was not only the result of my personal struggle to assert myself in Wilgenhof residence, but also because I was one of those described as "night disciples" by the writer F. Deist, a wavering believer who, like Nicodemus, approached Christ at night with his questions.

Since those early days, philosophy has come to be of great help to me. According to Professor Hennie Rossouw[1], one of my lecturers, the love of wisdom which is the basis of philosophy provides one with an "ethical navigation system" for orienting one's life. The purpose of philosophy is, after all, finding a viable way of life through reflection, a golden mean between the poles of "thought sclerosis", which results from a lack of thought, and "panic thinking" which results from being swamped by too many unanswerable questions.

In my 1985 study year this relationship between my religious questioning and philosophy was illustrated in an essay in which I drew a parallel between Nietsche's view of man (his idea of the "superman") and the Christian view of

---

1 Professor in philosophy during my student days at Stellenbosch University.

man created "in the image of God". I remember this essay in particular because it was one of the documents which had to be laboriously translated into English as a requirement for admission to a college at Oxford, a task complicated by the presence of a certain Melanie, sweetly working away at her first-year academic work at the desk of an absent room mate.

The "answers" in this essay soon proved to be no more than rather theoretical formulations at a rational level, yet it had a certain prophetic element, especially in terms of my three months in the Netherlands in 1986. An extract or two will show what I mean:

In his search for truth Nietzsche demonstrated vividly that Christianity as he experienced it was approaching God and therefore mankind WRONGLY. In Christian theology "God" was forged on the anvil of Platonic philosophy ... for this reason it is understandable that Zarathustra-Nietzsche turns away from the Forest-Saint worshipping his "God" on the mountain and proclaims the Uebermensch to the people at the marketplace in place of this dead God – people whose physical, material needs are disparaged in a Platonic, dualistic view of mankind which sees the soul as the essence of mankind.

Nietzsche's "God" is truly a "dead God", but still a "God" alive in our society. Too often our churches, our lives seem to be "sepulchers" of the "Heavenly Father" whom we worship on Sundays. It is often apparent from our work, political and especially sexual ethics that we do not only have a distorted image of God, but also a distorted image of man ...

Mercifully the Scriptures teach us that God has also accepted mankind's total depravity. So fully has He done this that He has erected the cross of Christ within this world with its Auschwitzes and Hiroshimas ... for this reason mankind can remain truly faithful to this earth – he must not be a dreamer or build castles in the air, but must realise Christ's victory on this earth ...

In the midst of all these questions and answers on the one hand and "good works" on the other, I did not take politics very seriously during my student years at Stellenbosch.

Certainly I was "against Apartheid" as were many of my white fellow students. In other words, it was clear to me at that stage that "separate development" as a policy could not work in practice. I duly voted "yes" in the 1983 (white) referendum in favour of "reforming" the lilywhite parliament. I could not fully grasp why the newly formed United Democratic Front was protesting so violently against this "step in the right direction". With several fellow young white South Africans I spoke out against secrecy within the Ruiterwag (an Afrikaner nationalist cultural/political organisation, also known as the "Junior Broederbond"). Along with several fellow Wilgenhof residents I even made a critical utterance or two in public, although within the safe confines of Stellenbosch.

My most daring "political" action during this time was probably the singing of our homemade Chancellor's Anthem to the tune of an old folksong at the annual Songfest in the Stellenbosch City Hall, admittedly protected by the anonymity of a whole gang of other Wilgenhoffers:

> Old PW[2] the clown
> Candidate for Chancellor
> without a BA to his name
> Dare we ask,
> is the Convocation mad ...
> or is PW perhaps
> a Broederbond buddy?
> Oh weep not,
> Do not mourn,
> Mike de Vries knows the score
> He has his reasons
> Don't you fear
> For nominating this silly ****!
> Hurrah for our apish Chancellor!

At the same time I can remember some other noises made by me in 1985 in the company of those self-same Wilgenhoffers. During supper, the news was broadcast of another "successful air-raid" on "ANC bases" in Botswana. I applauded with the rest of them, shouting "Hurrah for the SADF". After all, as I had remarked some years previously, we HAVE to defend our borders against numerous attacks by the terrorists ...

This superficial support for the political status quo of South Africa was partly the result of my attempts to escape from a politically charged name, partly due to peer pressure, partly the result of the carefree student life in a comfortably white Stellenbosch. My continued struggle for Jesus – perhaps not so much in my previous guise as SOLDIER – also played an important part.

2 PW Botha: President of (White) SA between 1978 and 1989.

My involvement in party politics (admittedly at the time I made no distinction between party politics and politics) was limited to attending a National Party Youth Branch camp during my first year. It was not so much the political part of the agenda that disturbed me, but rather the fact that there would have been no Sunday service that morning if I had not insisted on it. It did take place, although I had to be the "minister".

This incident confirmed my churchly scepticism regarding "dirty politics" and "corrupt politicians", at the same time reinforcing my faith in true reconciliation through the church. As late as 1985, during a visit to the Kwasisa Bantu mission station in Natal, I was in total agreement with the criticism of the (black and white) missionaries of the Tutus and Boesaks in our churches for their "excessive" political involvement. Long discussions with Fano Sibisi[3], in particular, in which he told me about the effect of the sanctions campaigns of Tutu and company on rural people, confirmed my rejection of party-political activism.

By the following year in Holland all my cherished convictions were being weighed and often found wanting. During my stay in Utrecht I was unexpectedly confronted with the distortions in my political "and especially sexual" ethics. I had to learn the hard way not just to write platitudes about "man in the midst of Auschwitz and Hiroshima" having to prevail in Christ. What about this particular person, Wilhelm Johannes Verwoerd, dreaming his Stellenbosch dreams barely a stone's throw from the black township, Kaya Mandi[4], and the "riven, dying world" on the Cape Flats?

This part of the story is probably best recounted by extracts from some of my letters to Melanie from Holland. Today I find these scribbled letters often painfully priggish and prissy, while Melanie is definitely anything but "my young girl-friend". I have resisted the temptation to correct my language and political utterances, which makes of these scrawled midnightly attempts at explaining to Melanie what foreign parts were doing to my thinking a reasonably reliable account of a crucial stage of my "Little Trek".

The extracts also provide background information to the stories which follow, especially regarding my relationship with Melanie. For this reason I want to dwell on a few letters and their account of a few other rebirths – taking place not far, incidentally, from where my grandfather and his grandfather and his grandfather were born.

3 Member of Kwasisa Bantu Mission station, KwaZulu/Natal province.
4 Literally "nice home/pretty place", impoverished township in Stellenbosch.

Little did I think while writing those letters that a prelude to my "journey through the world within" was already happening in the world out there in July 1986. It was during this time that I went to Utrecht on a study grant of the Netherlands South African Association (NZAV) to work on my MA thesis on "Humour and Suffering".

My first entry into the world outside the limits of Stellenbosch and the Cape was via Heathrow by aeroplane, from where I went to Oxford by car to visit my former English teacher, Mr David Taylor, for a few days.

From Oxford I made my own way to Utrecht, heavily laden with luggage full of useful and (mostly) useless baggage. At the end of my brief period in Holland I not only rid myself of much of the excess provisions, medicines, clothes and books in my luggage before returning home, but also the baggage of certain principles which had to be shed before I could crawl bit by bit through the eye of the needle.

During this time I painfully learnt to pray with the philosopher Johannes Degenaar (the Stellenbosch Socrates who was barred from the theological seminary in the sixties for fear of corrupting the young dominees with his ideas):

"Lord, you have come to teach us to turn people into Christians; now teach us how to turn Christians into people".

Letters from Abroad

76 Maurits Street
Thursday, 3 July 1986

Hi Melanie

I just feel like talking to you, this is the first chance I've had to sit down and write since arriving here yesterday. My room is on the first of three floors, at the back of the house and just above the kitchen, looking out on a little courtyard – seems like a real chaotic student house. Luckily it has a fridge, stove, cutlery and crockery.

Oh, yes, what I wanted to tell you – at dinner I met the other tenants: Johan Bouwer (doing a PhD in theology), his wife Amor and their son of two. (They are very friendly, but I miss some spirituality and warmth in them – small things, such as the way they treat the child, Amor's unladylike language. More than likely I am too quick to judge – I shall need a positive approach to get along with them.) Amor and Johan are really in charge of the house.

The other people are Rudolf Serfontein, a refined, slender chap studying piano teaching. (There goes the bell for ten o'clock. It's still broad daylight – thank goodness the church is so close.) He has odd ways, but I like him. The other chap is Steward van Wyk. He is a coloured from Swellendam. He helped me a lot this morning and then went to Amsterdam for the day.

Looking at the news tonight (every time, in fact) it felt so strange to see news about South Africa while overseas. The news does not seem to be slanted, but the problem is not so much what they broadcast, but what they leave out. Tonight there was an item on the twelfth bomb since the state of emergency (in Cape Town) and the fact that people ar still dying despite the state of emergency – some 100 in total since the proclamation.

A few hundred metres away there is a beautiful park (named after Queen Wilhelmina!) with giant, lovely trees, ponds with leaping fountains, attractive walking and cycling tracks and lots of geese, muscovy ducks and swans. There are even some goslings – so cute and fluffy, you simply want to pick them up.

[Barely a day later this romantic picture of Queen Wilhelmina Park was rudely shattered and this Wilhelm's relations with his housemates seriously complicated. Within the first few days my prudish soul was being confronted with thorny moral issues: not so much from my theological and philosophical books, but arising from intense discussions held with especially Amor and Rudolf. Thanks to these people at 76 Maurits Street I was forced to look anew at my personal AND political ethics. In the light of my history as Soldier for Jesus contemptuous of (party) politics, the combination of Amor (and Johan) and Rudolf was exactly the right medicine, although bloody bitter.]

76 Maurits Street
4 July 1986
8.25 pm

Hi there!

I am sitting in my room with a cup of black coffee and need to chat to you. A while ago I went jogging on foreign soil for the first time, and liked it a lot. (Not that much different to South Africa, can you believe it) ... I suppose familiarity will help me feel at home. I must say that after hearing Johan telling me about some of the things happening in Wilhelmina Park, I won't be able to feel this comfortable everywhere. It seems there was a homosexual rally of people from all over Europe and Britain — more than 6 000 in all! Apparently they showed their love for each other openly and unashamedly, some of the women were topless ... worst of what he saw was a SM chap parading around with an elastic band around his swollen willy. Wow! Funny how these things made me look differently at this beautiful spot. These things must happen all over the world (even in SA!); it's just curious to think of it happening so recently, so close by and in such a lovely spot ...

Maybe Amor and I are going to cross swords soon (she's doing a PhD in sociology) because she is rather left — she supports the ANC, economic boycotts etc. She is quite outspoken about people in SA who don't really know what's happening. I suppose she does (definitely) know more about it than me. What really gets me is the way she remarked this morning that she supports equality between the sexes. And often she doesn't dress Stian decently — he walks around the house with his bare bottom ...

There are many interesting and shocking publications on South Africa which are naturally banned down there. I will try to read them, such as the one I borrowed from Steward — poems by Dennis Brutus from Robben Island. (He was there as a political prisoner. It seems he's playing a major role in SA's sports isolation and as proponent of non-racial sport.)

11.55 pm
I would rather chat to you than listen to Amor and Johan outside my window (in the courtyard) arguing whether Johan is really an Apartheid theologian, whether

he acts out his choices vis à vis Apartheid ("*I had to kiss your arse to resign from the [white] Dutch Reformed Church ...*").

I don't know how to convey all this to you, how they accuse each other, whether she is really acting out her "*hatred for apartheid*" in the field of sociology (I can't believe they're both PhD students!). How can she ever be the wife of a minister and how could they serve a parish (of whatever church)? Is this gossiping, Melanie? I wanted to talk about it ...

The argument started when Johan and Rudolf began discussing satanism. Then Amor said that Johan and his church (who justified apartheid ideology theologically) were just as mistaken and benighted, that Christians were ignorant and that Johan was only feeling guilty about what his church was doing (or something like that). That was forty five minutes ago and now they're back at it again. Help!

... While listening to them (trying to read the Bible) I was thinking: one should pray for them and all the other fractured/foundering marriages and relationships with all our heart. We as Christians are wedded to Christ. How must his heart feel about people (us included) making statements about theologians and sociologists supporting devilish structures, but who do not give loving expression to our relationships with our spouses or neighbours? This may be the real tragedy (perhaps I am overreacting to what happened tonight, but it hurt me so deeply and set me to thinking about so many things). Perhaps this is why Christ said: "*First remove the beam from your own eye ...*"

76 Maurits Street
9 July 1986

Hullo there!

... this afternoon I visited the university library (De Uithof), but spent most of the time talking to Johan ...

Seems as if today is a day for exhausting discussion. While preparing supper, Amor and I started "chatting" about politics. At the start it did not feel like a real chat, more like one of our proper fights – far from a friendly exchange of ideas. It seemed to me she did not want to allow me to say what I wanted, or that she attacked and criticised me on every point for not being good enough and not showing enough solidarity with the suppressed blacks. I consequently tried to defend myself by criticising her views and gross generalisations about the Afrikaner and the Dutch Reformed Church. You must know that wound-up, tense, knot-in-the-guts feeling that comes from getting emotionally involved in an argument.

Well, after a lot of "chatting" an hour later I cooled down. I formed a better idea of her experiential background and past and decided she was really an honest sort of person, expressive, and not one to think calmly about things (like me? and you too, although I think you are more in her category). I was simply more prejudiced against her because of her harder, less refined personality than yours. Naturally I condemned her for the overheard "fight" of the other evening (I hope that letter did not upset you too much – just goes to show how wrongly you can judge people if you don't know them well) ...

What I really wanted to say is that I discovered in the course of the discussion that that was her way of showing how strongly she felt about something, not that she was attacking me personally and that I could learn a lot from her. I must admit that she was talking much more calmly towards the end. She has had a lot of contact with ANC members, with people of the Confessional Circle and Kairos (I know very little about them) and many blacks (members of the UDF) who felt oppressed in the SA context, especially by the SA government. In the process she developed an enormous antipathy towards the Afrikaner and the DRC. She has no desire for nuanced thinking, but will admit that things are not that simple. It is terribly important to her that we as whites must be critical of the injustices emanating from the Apartheid regime and the theological justification of this ideology. We cannot sit in our grand houses with huge salaries and mouth paternalistic criticism, but should prove our solidarity. (This is what blacks are also asking ... .) For instance, resign from the DRC, take part in the consumer boycott; these are the sort of things she was confronting me with.

I explained that I was countering apartheid and its effects within the structure (unacceptable to her, but we agree to differ on this) in a non-political way, inside the church, at a practical, inter-personal level (dialogue, ANC study tour last year, workers' camps, daily life), "apartheid" inside marriage and between family members included. She attaches more value to being involved in the struggle against unjust structures. In the end I realised that I was trying to exculpate myself and I wondered whether I was really prepared to sacrifice my privileged, peaceful, *comfortable lifestyle to assist the suffering and oppressed? Were we not trying to soothe ourselves with arguments, charity, not realising that for most blacks this was not enough? I finally realised that I needed to ask the Lord for forgiveness.*

The situation is so unbelievably complicated. There are so many factions in black ranks – with whom must I show solidarity? How to show solidarity with the oppressed without being alienated from my own people? Or does it mean here that the true imitation of Christ must cause a division between men and women, parents and children? (You know that section of the Scriptures don't you?) In other words, how far must one pursue reconciliation and when does it become self-protection and fear of really standing up for the truth?

I suppose you don't have any answers, but it is so difficult to be truthful with oneself and not to over-react – rather disturbing.

[The question of reconciliation and solidarity – my fear of alienating "my own people", the Afrikaner people and the Verwoerd family – are important themes on which I will expand in the following accounts. These first letters from Holland show that I experienced my exposure to other points of view primarily as a questioning of my Christian faith. The fact that my discussions during this crucial period were not held with "outsiders", but white, Afrikaans-speaking (former) DRC members, including a prospective minister like Johan, caught me unprepared. After all, the shield of this "Soldier of Jesus" was firstly designed to deflect the flaming darts of the "evil" (black) terrorists and Communists (and party politicians)!]

9 July 1986 (continued)

This afternoon Johan and I sat talking, he telling me about the crisis facing the Scriptural profession in Europe, with hardly any givens, how our interpretation of the Scriptures has become so relativised and contextualised, that I wondered what had happened to simple childlike faith. Also the whole issue of "anonymous Christianity", namely that we should not arrogantly assume the right to proclaim Christ's final judgment.

Do you remember our chats about the question of mission work among the Muslims? I realised anew that the motivation for mission work dare not be judgmental (the people here lack any sense of sin or guilt as it is), but that we as the church have a message of love which must help people to live a truly human life on this earth. This inevitably brings one to the whole question of God and suffering, to unjust, oppressive structures, famine, unemployment. In other words, horizontally, in an inter-personal level, what is the active, liberating (not only spiritually either!) role of the church and Christians? Can you remember what Leonardo Boff (the South American liberation theologian) said, that God is present where people were liberated from political oppression (and often from the hierarchical, status quo maintaining church, i.e. the Catholic Church – and the DRC?) We must pray hard for the coming synod! The people here are expecting (or hoping for) a schism, for more clarity on where the DRC really stands. I don't know what to think.

Johan also said (criticising the church here) that not enough is being made of the vertical relationship between the believer and God. Apparently the people in this secularised society have a tremendous need for experience of and contact with the transcendental/God. There is apparently massive growth in Eastern, mystical religions – there is a meditation centre in our street.

Another subject we discussed was homosexuality and its Scriptural justification (for instance where Christ says "... some were created not to be married ..."). What really disturbs me is that Rudolf himself is gay. But that's not the real problem – I like him a lot. The point is he cannot believe in a God who rejects his sexual disposition. In other words, telling him I think it is wrong in principle without condemning him doesn't help, neither does telling him he should change. Do you see the problem? This is something which will require a lot of reading by both of us. It is so endlessly complicated. I am grateful this is not my first exposure to the problem (over here they don't talk of normal and homosexual people, but of homos and heteros). How does one reject it in principle, while still making these people welcome in the church?

Another tricky issue was whether women in a lesbian marriage (the feminine partner) should be artificially or even naturally inseminated. Apparently a significant proportion of children from such marriages are also homosexual and the boy children are better able to control their emotions. What do you think?

Another issue (how many more?) was pre-marital sex, which is not taboo to Christians over here. In a relationship, not necessarily with the intended spouse, it is a perfectly normal method of communication. Wow, this really sounds unac-

21

ceptable, but I know it won't be easy when one starts discussing it with these Christians. Are the Scriptures really that clear about what a marriage is? I (we) will have to read and think and talk about this a lot. (Don't you worry now!)

They all want to go down the road for some coffee/beer. I will tag along for the company. So, bye for now ... I've given you a lot to think about. You must read up, I need your help!

[The next letter illustrates my incredible gullibility vis-à-vis the "Government" (with a capital G) and especially the "Security" Police. Most of the people involved were after all Afrikaners, "my" people: my best friend Gawie's parents were close friends of "Oom Dawie" (De Villiers) and "Oom Gerrit" (Viljoen, then both NP Cabinet ministers); my brothers and friends went off to do their military duty without demur. My injured back kept me out of the army, but the year before I was also applauding the Security Force for another attack on an "ANC base".]

76 Maurits Street
Thursday, 10 July 1986

Hullo my angel!

I am writing to you about all the things I heard today. What a disturbing climax to a disturbing day! I wish you could have been here to hear everything and to decide with me what is true or not.

Amor and Johan started telling me about all the information they have picked up from banned publications, magazines and from discussions with exiles, ANC supporters. It is simply SHOCKING! It deals with the diabolical role of the Security Police, in fact with all security organisations such as the KGB, CIA, about everything going on underground (literally and figuratively).

(During the conversation a friend of Rudolf's came visiting. Seems to me they intend to spend the night together! Perhaps they are only friends. His excitement about the visit of his friend is a curious experience ...)

I don't know what to believe of everything they tell me, but it seems quite certain that the phone here is tapped – information reaches her mother without being written or told, letters are opened, things such as films are removed and never reach friends or parents, Amor is often tailed when she goes to town to meet ANC people. According to her uncle in the Security Police, files are kept on everyone going overseas (especially to the Netherlands), their movements are monitored. Apparently there are files on just about every white in any sort of leadership position ...

They also talked about visiting a woman in the Netherlands. She is an ANC member as well as a devoted Catholic and opposes violence. This woman told and showed them how the Security Police tortured her — for instance, they stuck wires under her nails, into her ears (she is still hard of hearing) and up her vagina to shock her and obtain information. (I hope I'm not telling you too much — perhaps you should keep this to yourself.)

I found a book here written by a friend of Steve Biko's (one Donald Woods, who fled SA). Woods tells who Biko was — seems to me he was a wonderful leader and person — and how he was murdered. There are photographs of what his body looked like and where he had been hit. According to the police he died of a heart attack. There is also a long list of people who died in detention — according to the Security Police most of them hanged themselves or had accidents, such as "slipping on cakes of soap".

These are only some of the things we discussed. (This book is naturally banned in SA. Woods smuggled the manuscript out.) I really don't know what to think, I don't know how I'm going to feel after reading it. I wish you could read it too — if you're found in possession of this book in SA it may mean six months in jail. Perhaps I should buy it and take it to England for you to read.

Amor and Johan say that eventually they didn't know who to believe — perhaps just God! — and that they have lost all their naivety about the NP government and all its claims about good intentions. According to reliable information the Security Police even have their own "hit squad" (ex-recces) (special forces) who are paid to liquidate opponents of the NP. They mentioned some examples of murders which remained unsolved or were never even investigated. I can't tell how true that is (I spoke to Mr Taylor in Oxford about a Dr Smit or some such person who had been inexplicably murdered, one of the names mentioned by Amor).

So, what is one to say of all this? As Johan remarked: "Cry, the beloved country!". If you take all these things seriously you will go mad or paranoid. It is such a strange feeling, so whether everything is true or not, some parts are surely true: the doctors who examined Biko were found guilty after all, there are some eyewitness accounts etc. I don't know whether I should use all the opportunities to gain this sort of information. It must make one interpret things differently. Perhaps I should write to Professor Willie Esterhuyse[5] for advice. Apparently the government is also involved in several secret projects of which the public know nothing.

How does one keep a cool head through all this? How does one digest this sort of information; is it digestible at all? How does one keep being honest to oneself and investigate everything in searching for the truth? One thing – maybe two – I will adhere to: all this rubbish will not come between you and me. We will have to process it together, live with it and fulfil our limited (non-political) role. We will have to be much more critical (in all directions). This South Africa I'm learning about is just so different!

Secondly, it must not come between me and the Lord and a naive, childlike faith in His victory over Evil! It simply shows me the immense power and influence of Evil over the world. Perhaps we have not taken it seriously enough up to now, what do you think? Let me put it like this: the violence from the side of the government may let us better understand Amor's radicalness (and that of the ANC). Johan admires the ANC's patience for waiting so long before resorting to violence. We must never become like that! But how does one remain serious without losing a sense of playfulness, joy, hope, humour? (You don't have to answer all these questions!)

Eyes shut now: "Lord, I dedicate myself and Melanie to you ALL OVER. I don't know how to make sense out of all the things I have heard and will hear, but Lord, help us in our lack of faith! Please, Lord – things can't be that complicated. Please reveal Yourself to us, clearly and forcefully. You have arisen, You did give us the Holy Spirit. Death, where is your sting?"

PS: I have just made a cheese sandwich – eating it now (nice) – and started thinking, you'll simply have to understand. Don't think I'm silly or just say: "Never mind, it's not that bad". (Which is true, but don't say it!). I must be silly after all ... off to bed with me.

1.30 am
Lying in bed and trying to pray a lot of things entered my mind. I started

---

5 Professor in philosophy and business ethics, University of Stellenbosch; prominent political commentator.

wondering if I wasn't being silly to write all those things to you, whether I wasn't overreacting. Maybe it is simply the shock of meeting another world inside SA.
I thought again about what Gerrit Viljoen said: "There can be no reform without order; reform goes hand in hand with stability". But neither the ANC nor the Security Police are angels. The tragedy of Apartheid is that lofty good intentions are sunk by civil servants down below. How is a state to guarantee its safety? Where does one draw the line? Are all the government's reforms really pointless, cosmetic or irrelevant? Is there so much evil in everything the government and Christians in the government are doing? (Am I being naive?). What about black people like Fano Sibisi of Kwasisa Bantu who are not as critical of the Government?
Yet the tragedy of innocent people being tortured in the most gruesome fashion by the Security Police remains. Do the people in top government, Gerrit Viljoen or Dawie de Villiers, know about it?
On the other hand: Amor and company may not be that innocent either. What responsibility does the state for instance have to protect its security against subversive literature? And who determines what is subversive?
And again: what gives this government the right to restore citizenship to blacks without ever having the right to take it away? Why did the DRC not earlier listen to critics of apartheid?
What about many people of conservative political views, who are committed Christians, such as my Uncle Carel Boshoff, my mother, Granny Smit? Did my grandfather not know about all these things? According to my father he was a well-loved Minister of Native Affairs. Or is my and their image of him the result of one-sided indoctrination? Does each of us (all the whites) bear a collective responsibility for everything the Security Police have done or are doing? Then surely we are guilty of all the wrongs done by everyone.
Am I rationalising? How does one reconcile the different worlds in South Africa? Especially where the government acts and thinks from one world, the First World in conflict with the Third World. Everything is getting theoretical again.
Sorry if I'm tiring you out! Maybe I should try to get some sleep.

[I wonder now how much sleep I would have got then if Amor and company had not shown me only the iceberg's tip. At a recent meeting she told me about a visit from the Security Police while still in South Africa. In order to "encourage" Amor to stop her "devious activities" they stuck Stian's finger into a meat grinder...

But let me return rather to my feelings at the time, my crisis of faith about SA's politics ... and Rudolf's homosexuality.]

76 Maurits Street
12/7/86
3.20 pm

... I wanted to respond to all you wrote about the bombs and Nelson Mandela and the hungry children. It is unbelievably difficult to know what to do in practice about all this destruction. The other day (evening rather) I tried to explain and afterwards thought about it again. I am happy to be confronted with all this "banned" information, although I am hesitant to read the Biko book. When you've read or heard about something like this, you want to ask whether there is anything left that's nice, can one really laugh and joke and enjoy life when so many people are suffering? The other I day I told Amor about how beautiful the snow on the Jonkershoek mountains was, when she wondered aloud whether the people of Crossroads without warm clothes in their tin shacks would find it beautiful.

I know she isn't right, but I also realise that I don't have the answer. It's almost as if it's easier not to hear about all the suffering on earth. But then I think about how Christ mingled with the whores and sinners, how they turned to Him, that Christ lived out His message of hope in a time of poverty, political injustice, religious hypocrisy, moral decay. The trouble is, I don't always know how to follow Him! He was often so radical: what are the implications of some of His advice: "sell what you own" ... "who does not hate his brother or family or wife ..." "render unto Caesar" ... "two commandments" etc. Then I wonder whether we ever shouldered our responsibility and involvement (not only money!) in Stellenbosch as we should have. What more could we do? Where do you draw the line? Maybe it is because we discussed it so often before I left, what it means to dedicate one's self, money and possessions to the Lord, especially after what has happened in Cape Town. (Amor asked me whether I gave up any of my time to help.) This isn't meant as criticism!

The other matter which disturbs me is Rudolph's homosexuality, which he pro-

claims so freely (as do so many others here). I wonder whether these people wouldn't also feel drawn to Christ (like the whores – in fact I'm sure of it). But what about our Church's loveless condemnation? Can I feel free to invite him to become a Christian? What about all the condemnation? What if he was born like that – which is what I suspect?

[My growing friendship with Amor did not mean that she left me alone – quite the contrary. She also studied philosophy at Stellenbosch, with the same lecturers I had. Like Socrates – gadfly of the Greeks – she could also poke a few holes into a few more of the dykes surrounding this Stellenbosch "soldier" and student. This time the question marks weren't being raised around prominent people in the DRC, the "Government" or the "Security Police", but mentors whose political wisdom I valued highly.]

76 Maurits Street
16/7/1986
1 am

Hello Melanie!

Seems as if it's going to be one of our late night (early morning) chats. I have another batch of things to discuss with you while sorting them out for myself – probably not possible at all, seeing it's all about politics again!
    Now the problem is conscientious objection. This is where it started – I mean the political part of the discussion – as Amor and Rudolph and Johan (mainly Amor and I) sat chatting in the courtyard from 8 pm.
    Perhaps I should explain how we got there. I don't agree with everything she says, but I have heard some clever arguments. I don't want to sound too clinically rational about the matter, but this may make it easier to sort out the emotions. It is a strange feeling: I do not have the answers to their questions and what I hear is disturbing – I could quite easily agree with her. But it is as if I "know" (in my heart) that this is not the only interpretation, that I can't go along with everything. I wish I had more facts at my disposal – perhaps I should, no wait, I think I must write to Gawie[6] or Prof. Willie or Fano (or all of them). Prof. Willie may be the

---
6 Gawie de la Bat, a close friend at that time and fellow theological student at the University of Stellenbosch.

best bet, or what?

(Amor and Co. are not impressed with him — she calls him a two-face for belonging to the Broederbond[7] while making all those enlightened pronouncements. She can't stand him. She also dislikes Prof. Hennie for "his part in maintaining the White Afrikaner identity of Stellenbosch".)

That is where the discussion started: She said she had no respect for Prof. Hennie as a person due to all these things (although she respects his philosophical abilities). I then tried to explain that while I did not agree with everything he said or did I still respected him as a person and that this respect will have a bearing on the way I will differ from him (if at all). She then wanted to know how far I was prepared to defy his authority. What it was really all about was how far I was prepared to stand up for the values I believed in.

... I have just become aware that I haven't really thought through the consequences of my political convictions. I have concentrated so much more on Christian values and convictions — "freedom of speech" is simply not as important to me as "love for your marriage" or "loyalty". Maybe there is something to be said for both of these, if they are at all separable...

Then again there are MANY non-political problems which need specialised attention for which I must train myself. Many blacks, "radical" whites in SA and overseas, concentrate too much on the political problems and the dehumanising effects of a repressive society, separated families, torture of women, even children! (By the way, apparently many children under 11 are being held in SA. Last year a two-year old and three-and-a-half year old died in detention! That Mrs Mabata's child starved to death with her ... "She was a Commie, wasn't she?" is what the policeman apparently said.) Amor says information about this is available at the British Council in London. The problem in SA (like elsewhere) is who to believe. Sometimes, if not often, it seems as if the world outside aren't that mistaken.

In the end we agreed that you could or had to become a heart surgeon, but that you still had to live according to your convictions. We are trying, aren't we Melanie? We just have so much to learn. Or should we rather keep right out of the "struggle"? What would Christ have done? His disciples included a Zealot and a publican.

Then we got to conscription and the whole question: who does one fight against? Is the Communist onslaught really that bad, or is it mostly propaganda?

---

7 Literally "league of Brothers", an elitist, Afrikaner Nationalist secret society which became very influential and controversial during the National Party's 46 years in power.

All the countries around SA (except South West Africa/Namibia) support the ANC, in other words if they should come into power, we won't really need a defence force. (I'm oversimplifying the discussion!) The SA government's incursions into neighbouring countries, even as far as Tanzania, are destabilising. We also talked about the whole question of whether the ANC did have any alternative to violence – my question is whether violence has to include bombing soft targets.

I really don't know how to tell you about all this. The whole thing of "Americanism" I found just as disturbing: the double morality of the US – people fleeing to the Netherlands, for instance as a result of "Big Brother" (the extended US security network); the US military involvement in many South American countries. What I'm trying to say is that I'm picking up a different perspective from them on the US for instance. Also on the so-called "civilised" mentality which pronounces on "African barbarism" (necklacing) while itself developing chemical or nuclear weapons which destroy men, women, children, the environment!

What is one to say of all these things? I hope you don't think me stupid to listen to them, or that they might be naive or stupid. I am worried that one could say, "They don't know the facts, they are over-reacting, they are one-sided" and then it turns out to be quite different after all!

I suppose it does one good to be confronted with new ideas, don't you? I just wish I could discuss them with you right now. Neither of us really knows enough and we are so gullible...

In the final analysis I just feel, "Fine! Let's stop talking and get involved in all the suffering around us, let us seek the Lord with all our hearts. Isn't that the secret of Fano and his people? Or are they again not politically involved enough? Is that sufficient proof of 'solidarity'?"

Well, we wanted to be philosophical; we love questioning things and seeking the truth.

It's almost half-past three, so maybe I should turn in. Trouble is, I'm wide awake.

[All this lack of sleep naturally meant that my MA thesis, the ostensible reason for my visit, did not progress much. I never regretted this, because I learnt much more from the people at 76 Maurits Street. The following few letters seem like a deviation from the main account of my development from "soldier for Jesus" to a "tree in the wind", a central theme in my decision to join the ANC. Looking back, I now realise not only how important it was for me to be shocked by Amor's politics, but at the same time, from my relationship with Rudolf, to have radical doubts about what it meant to be a "soldier for Jesus". Given my ideal at the time to become a pastoral psychologist/marriage counsellor, it shook me to my foundations to discover that my fairly confident black-and-white, soldier-for-Jesus, DRC revulsion for "filthy" homosexuality was in contradiction to the heart of the Christian Gospel. It was as if walls around my unconditional love for my neighbour had to be flattened. This traumatic experience also reinforced the arguments of Amor and co. about my political home also being built on sand. However, it would still need a lot of demolition work and reconstruction before I, with dirtied hands, would join in and help build Albert Luthuli's ideal of a "home for all" in South Africa.]

76 Maurits Street
17/7/86
15h00

Hello my little girl!

... this is a funny time of day to be writing a letter, but after the "depression" of the last few days, I just feel like a chat – I miss your face and your advice and good spirits.

Do you know, I don't mind if we are "socialised", "conservative" or whatever, but I am very glad that you are a gentle, feminine feminist. I suppose you can guess what Amor and I and Rudolf have just been discussing.

We really only chatted. I surprise myself – after the political discussion the other day, which kept me up so late, writing letters and disturbing my sleep, I went through a strangely "depressive", introspective period where I did not want anything to do with them and where they irritated me immensely. I know I am overreacting, that I am criticising them unfairly, that I should not judge them, but I simply don't feel like it! All these strange thoughts go whirling through my head: "You can go to hell". Then I try to tell myself rationally that I'm being silly, but to no avail. Last night (11 pm) I went cycling just to get out. It helped, but when I returned to my room and wanted to turn in, they were still sitting outside my window, discussing politics and feminism. I switched on my radio, but I could still hear their voices in the background. It was immensely irritating. It was such a trapped feeling, because I had nowhere else to go. Then I started reading and praying, but it did not help, I kept feeling more frustrated. Well, when they finally went to bed I was wide awake and rolled around in bed for a long time. On top of it the weather was hot and muggy. I really longed for you ...

I wanted to tell you about all the things we talked about: Rudolf said something about being "homophile" and I asked him how it differed from being "homosexual". Then we started talking about those things in general and the influence AIDS has had on the movement. Apparently "homophile" (love of men) is the nice term as used by the Church for instance. In fact there is no difference, and as Rudolf says, he knows of no "homophiles" who don't also have sexual relations. I still find it uncomfortable to hear someone speaking so openly about all these things and his sexual activities.

In the USA there is a wave of AIDS hysteria and people tend to be less forthright about their sexual disposition. It seems AIDS isn't simply a disease for which homosexuals are responsible. Apparently it has been around for years (medical science just did not have a name for it) and originates from Africa, where homosexuality is uncommon. According to Rudolf there isn't much difference between male and female homosexuals, between "fags" and "dikes" or gays and lesbians (women are no more gentle than men, says he, this idea is simply the result of socialisation). Radical lesbians propound suppression of men (as countermeasure). These people are apparently quite frightening and easily recognisable. Rudolf and Amor suggested that I look in at some or other nightclub!

76 Maurits Street
31/7/86
9.30 pm

Hi there!

Wow! WISH you were here. I did not want to write this, because I feel we often say it without it helping; in fact it makes things worse. But now I really mean it. I have so many things and experiences inside me that I simply have to talk to you, but I don't know where to start.

... maybe it has something to do with my circumstances here in this house, between Amor and Rudolf and the environment – criticism of South Africa; strange, unsettling experiences, hearing and seeing things from a different world, another perspective, all this openness about sexuality, feminism, the female (and male) body and in particular homosexuality ...

This evening I went to town at about 7.30, it being "koopavond" (late night shopping) again. So I went to a bookshop to look at a few theological and philosophical books. They also had a section on sexual issues. I looked for books on homosexuality in particular. I found a book on the admissions and struggles of some 50 Catholic lesbian nuns, which was rather disturbing. This set me to thinking about Rudolf and Pieter (his friend) who apparently wanted to bath together at 3 am! This showed me again how little I understand of this world. I got quite despondent thinking about how one day I wanted to help people with sexual problems inside and outside marriage ...

Regarding politics, I think I must first send you some of the articles I have read. Also the "open letter" written by Andre P Brink to the State President, which is rather depressing, especially with Amor's despondent commentary on it. Then I realise everything is not really so simple, although I don't always have answers. Then I wonder whether Fano and other positive blacks really know what is happening, for instance in Soweto and other cities where the real and relevant unrest is taking place.

11.55 pm

Hello my angel!

Now I feel a LOT better. Just before starting to write to Gawie it suddenly occurred to me (seeing Rudolf coming up the stairs as I was fetching some tea) to ask him to recommend some of his reading matter to me, as I wanted to learn more about "homophilia". He gave me a few magazines on homosexual subjects. These seem to be very explicit about subjects like "safe sex", "homosexual theatre", "Lesbian relations: the longer, the sweeter!", "Enchanted by male beauty", "Women and AIDS" to name a few from the covers. I think I will read some, because he thinks "Homologie" is the best in the world of lesbians and gays. I feel as if liberated after talking to him. We chatted about politics too and agreed that it is easy to criticise SA, but that very few people are really prepared to get involved. The Netherlands and Britain in particular have a rather sordid colonial past and are now saddled with guilt complexes.

Nicest of all was that I could talk to him and question him on homosexuality; that I stopped wondering and being cautious and that I can now discover as much as possible on the subject and gather information that I (we!) could also use in SA where it is not available. I shall try to tell you as much as possible, because I already know many things are going to disturb me. But it doesn't help to run away. I believe one should try to bring the Gospel to these people somehow without telling them to change, **without** condemning them for their sins.

This is different to what I think about it now, because then it is no longer a matter of being "normal" to be heterosexual and "abnormal" to be homosexual. I don't know how you are going to get around some parts of Scripture (Christ as the Groom and the Church as the bride, for instance), but there are so many thousands of people having this sexual orientation who don't want to be or can't be any different. Is it not in the final analysis all about the quality of love, for instance in a homosexual marriage? In 1 Cor. 13 it is not just about heterosexual love. The image of the Groom and Bride conveys a message of trust and dedication, not necessarily one of man-woman sex. Do those parts of Scripture condemning sodomy not refer to sinful lust, immorality etc. and not necessarily to a solemn, faithful homosexual relationship? Did God not make us free to choose, together with the responsibility (according to the Ten Commandments) it brings? What about a fine, pure homosexual relationship against a faithless heterosexual one? Is the criterion not something more than mere sexual orientation?

I'm going for some tea now, thinking about how the two of us are now entering an area about which we know so little, but about which so many prejudices exist (even in us) but which will be of great relevance in the ministry one day. So few people can speak with any authority or frankness about it. Imagine the plight of homosexual people in a community (church!) which is prejudiced and uncharitable ...

76 Maurits Street
6/8/86
10.30 pm

Hi there, my love!!!

If you could only know how I miss you tonight. It is almost painful ... I suppose it does one good to be alone for a while, although it looks like a case of "Severe Mercy", with more of the former. Faith teaches us to rely on the latter, not so? We believe that there is a God, a Power which stands above mere reality. A Power which is not Fate, but a PERSON who made us out of LOVE and who stays with us.

It's just so difficult to believe this sometimes. Especially after a day like today in Amsterdam (with its heat and hunger), with all those thousands of people leading a Godless life it seems – especially the young ones with their weird dress and hairdos and curiously cold expressions; all the sex shops and sex supermarkets row after row – even a "Sex Museum" with all those revolting pictures in the windows; all the people (chaps and their girls) looking at all this and laughing. (I wonder how I/we would have been if we had grown up in an open society like this.)

... and then Amor wanted to talk politics again tonight. Unfortunately I told her about a chat I had this afternoon with a Chicagoan who is connected to a Catholic university with the responsibility for foreign investments ($400 million!). He was sounding off about all the big corporations who pay their workers so little and exploit them. I did not feel so good after that.

I happened to ask someone this morning which tram to catch and it turned out to be this friendly Catholic. When he heard that I came from South Africa and that I wanted to become a DRC minister, he really wanted to chat. He has a real understanding of the complexity of our situation. He supports sanctions and disinvestment (a big issue in the USA at the moment) but only in part. He feels that some of the large US corporations in South Africa, such as Coke and General Motors, are doing good work such as fostering non-racialism in the workplace, in housing.

I am almost inclined to agree with him, because sanctions are the only non-violent means of applying pressure to the government. Some blacks like Tutu are also asking for it. On the other hand I still agree with what Fano said about double standards of people like Boesak and Tutu, the dependence of families in the *countryside, like KwaZulu, on jobs for their men in the cities and the effect of sanctions on these people. What I'm trying to say is that here we have serious talk about sanctions and that countering the argument is not that easy, especially because there are many whites happily living their luxurious lives without worrying too much about the plight of blacks. Perhaps one only hears certain groups more than others.*

I wonder how it would have been if I had not shared a house with Amor and had not been confronted with their points of view. Radicalism is just so tiring, especially when it emanates from a strong-willed person like her. It is much more difficult than I thought "working" with radicals. And she isn't even black! ...

76 Maurits Street
7/8/86
17h30

Hello there!

Just a quick hello before I start working. Today is/was one of those days – I feel listless and up to nothing at all. Do you feel like this sometimes? ... Perhaps this is one of the things I simply have to learn to deal with, as part of all these new experiences, but mostly being alone, especially when I spent a day among people as the ones in Amsterdam yesterday ...

After reading the Bible this morning, I just got back into bed. Amor noticed that I was out of sorts and brought me some tea in bed a little later. We had a long chat, and I felt a lot better! This is something one could learn from her, the trouble she goes to when she notices something is not what it should be. I felt bad about how critical I had been of her. We talked at length about emotional support, how we as Christians owed it to one another, but that we so seldom succeed, because when we don't agree about politics, we cut each other off so easily and are not prepared to love our "enemies". We still have a lot to learn about simple, practical Christianity, don't we?

76 Maurits Street
15/9/86
01h05

My dear heterosexual, Christian, chaste companion!
I can only laugh about the house I'm living in, especially with the new lodgers who have moved in.
When you look at all the sexual orientations which I have to deal with/confront here gathered under one roof, my prissy little soul freaks out: a homosexual quite actively engaged in his love affair with a "liefjonge" (who is bisexual and has a girl-friend!), two lesbians (Karin and Mandy – I learnt this tonight) who are also quite active (i.e. are having a love affair), and a young man sleeping with his girl. Amazing! And that after two months with a fiery ANC supporter and her equally critical husband!
Tonight it really tickled my fancy: this innocent, protected, Afrikaner, DRC theological student suddenly in the middle of this highly diverse "den of lions". I wish you were here to share it all!
(I think I am able to laugh – especially with Rudolf – because, although I can't agree with what they do, I cannot condemn them emotionally; I am able to look beyond his/her/their sexual orientation and that is so liberating. I was able to tell Rudolf this tonight and he said he did not find me judgmental at all.)
Best of all was that I felt for the first time tonight that I could start talking to Rudolf about my understanding of the Gospel of Jesus Christ – not just to still my "confessing conscience" (which has been bothering me) but because I want to, because I love him ...
This is a wonderful feeling – I may not have progressed much with my MA thesis during these three months, but the Lord has taught me an immense amount about people, about my own blindness and prejudices and emotional inabilities, my lack of true charity in spite of who or what my neighbour is.
(It is not as if I am making a great success of it; it's simply that I am much clearer about what we should strive towards – it's so liberating! As if all this light reveals the darkness in me, our church, our people, at the same time lighting everything up. As if I can so clearly see how I have grown (in terms of "sexual thinking" but also politically) but how different it would have been if I had not

been living in this house with these (South African) people. It was incredibly tough at the beginning, and still is, but it is as if the shackles of prejudice are dropping off. I know that these changes will make an unbelievably big difference to my life (wherever and however it proceeds), that they will create more problems and hardship and conflict (especially in SA) but that there is so much certainty that this is the right direction. I hope it doesn't sound arrogant. Do you understand?)

It really felt tonight as if Rudolf was opening up and that I saw for the first time how he thought and felt: how he had suffered even as a child by having a father who would not accept or understand him; a father whom Rudolf hated for as long as he can remember, and how this hate grew to include all fathers in the family, in the nation, especially the church (my, our church!) because they also rejected him. How since coming to Holland he had to learn to deal with his new rights and freedoms as well as his new, strange relationship with Pieter. How he often doesn't really know where he is heading, that he often feels his life is without meaning.

It is incredibly difficult talking to him about Christ, because to him the church where he met this Christ is the church which murdered Christ for him, which blunted his emotions for any Christian values, message as a result of all his strong negative associations with the Afrikaans DRC.

This is more or less what Nietszche said too: "God is dead ... the churches are the sepulchres ..." Rudolf's life is the proof that Nietszche wasn't that far wrong, but the tragedy is that it is not the true, living God who has been declared or experienced as "dead", but much rather an idol who we pray to and propagate.

Karen and Mandy I need to get to know (much) better, although it is as if my traumatic experience with Rudolf has opened me up ...

76 Maurits Street
18/9/86
13h15

Hi there!

... this must be one of the most wonderful things I have learnt the past few months (after much struggling and uncertainty). Last night reading the parable of the Good Samaritan it struck me like a blow: I often act, due to my own moral

37

schemes, my Christian sense of right and wrong, just like the Pharisee and the Levite! It is not easy to admit this to myself, but that in effect is what is happening. This is how other people standing outside my view of what is right see it. But this is NOT what Christ did! He taught me not to judge, which does not mean a laissez-faire acceptance and approval of all that is wrong. It requires of me to see my brothers and sisters in all the gluttons, boozers, whores and homosexuals and Pharisees (theological students?).

The mystery (heart) of Christianity seems to me that Christ identified with sinful humanity to such an extent that He could say: "Insofar as you have done it to the least, you have done it to ME". The essence is surely "that God so loved the world" and that is what I must convey. I know this love is associated with holiness, with punishment for sin and that God demands perfect honesty, purity, love. The problem is that I am so principled, that I enjoy it so much being a chosen one, morally superior, educated, civilised that I have no more charity. This is hypocrisy. Perhaps Christ will say one day: "I was a prostitute, I cohabited, I was a homosexual and you did not visit Me ..."

[Shortly before I left for Holland I met a former British ambassador, Archie McKenzie and his wife Ruth, in Stellenbosch. I was deeply impressed by their combination of political involvement and dedicated Christianity. I consequently did not forget their invitation to a Moral Rearmament conference in Switzerland. After two harrowing months in Maurits Street it was refreshing to spend five days in a beautifully renovated hotel a thousand metres above Lake Geneva and take part in a "Dialogue between the Continents". In the process a few more prejudices were destroyed and new friendships forged. My letters also tell the embarrassing story of visitors from the Cape who came "to put South Africa's case", in the process demonstrating all my Afrikaans, white political prejudices. I am also not so sure whether moral "rearmament" was always that beneficial in "disarming" this "Soldier for Jesus", whether MRA did help me overcome my distaste for dirty politics.]

*Caux
20/8/86
11h30*

Hello Melanie

Since arriving here yesterday (since I've been overseas really!) I've had such an urge to "chat" to you about everything happening around me ...

... you know, it's really a wonderful experience to meet so many people from so many different countries – last weekend there were people from some 53 countries! Apart from those I met yesterday there was a minister from Tanzania, a businessman from Pakistan, someone from Fiji. This morning there were people from Uruguay, Puerto Rico, Cyprus and Kenya, sharing their experiences about "From Fear to Victory". Tonight I am dining with a man from the Philippines. He is involved in resettling Indo-Chinese refugees – a wonderful Christian who has seen difficult times and who has been actively involved in the anti-Marcos resistance movement. I'm looking forward to that. Tomorrow night I dine with the McKenzies from Scotland. Last night at dinner with five young people and an elderly lady from Holland, it was interesting to discover that the six of us represented five continents: a man from Australia; a young committed Christian Californian; Johannes de Pous and the other lady from Holland; a young farmer from southern Italy, and myself from Africa!

Places previously only heard of suddenly stopped being just a dot on a lifeless map and became countries with problems, people, natural beauty. In bed last night I saw the world atlas in front of me – suddenly all the countries came alive: lights came on, swarms of people, cars. Then I suddenly realised how small and insignificant we all are, how each person's world can so easily become THE world – as if you/I sometimes want to claim God as our own, the feeling of being God's favourite ...

*Caux
21/8/86
14h40*

Hi there!

As you may guess things are going well with me. I am really surprised to feel so much at home and that I have the confidence to speak to so many people.

This afternoon I was talking to the McKenzies about South Africa and the future (for instance, the DRC general synod and its political implications) and I suddenly realised how dark one can let everything appear. How gloomy it is, how unbelievably complex everything is, especially in politics. (What does Prof Willie say? They know him too and talk of his important role as intermediary between the government and black people.)

Then Mrs McKenzie repeated something said by Frank Buchman (founder of MRA and devoted Lutheran minister), namely that if you are in a crisis (especially a political one) that is the time to influence people around you, to draw them closer to Christ, even if it happens one by one. That is how Christ worked – the woman at the well, Zacchaeus. Then He was being truly revolutionary; then He expected a change of heart in that person, a complete abnegation from the self and a complete dedication to the service of God and his or her neighbour.

The same idea arose in the film we saw yesterday, which was made in Nigeria 30 years ago. It deals with various political parties and their leaders, each trying to gain political power, the underlying struggle, hatred, conniving etc. The premier then visits a World Conference in Geneva where he discovers God and the MRA's four principles of "absolute love, honesty, purity, unselfishness" (a summary of the Sermon on the Mount). He realises that before the political revolution can occur, God expects a revolution in our hearts, through which we are to be freed from hatred, bitterness, impurity; that we forgive one another even if we feel ourselves to be the aggrieved party. This man then applies those principles in his marriage and in politics and only then finds true freedom.

The other film to which I have already referred, "For the Love of Tomorrow" tells the poignant story of Irene Laure, a Frenchwoman active in the Resistance during World War 2 and bearing bitter hatred against the Germans (she was here last week although very old now). At a conference in Caux and in intense struggle with God (she wanted to leave when 150 Germans attended) she realised that she could not strive for reconciliation and peace in the world while bearing so much bitterness in her own heart. Eventually she went so far as to ask for forgiveness in the large hall of 600 people (Germans included) and literally to offer the hand of reconciliation. After this she visited Germany numerous times and did wonderful work.

It was truly touching to see how the Lord used her. If you were to see the film you would never doubt the indispensable role to be performed by women in our society as well. I felt excited on your behalf and about your future struggle for "women's rights"!

I can't tell you now what MRA is and what I think about it all ... I am not quite clear about how everything works, especially because Muslims too are confessing about how it works in their lives. But if you listen to the testimony of Christians in particular, it really sets you to thinking. I was surprised about how critical and suspicious I (and our church?) am and wonder whether one shouldn't say "who is not with Me, is against Me"...

Seems as if my time is up ... thanks for the chat and don't worry about me losing my way among all these "moralists" – quite the opposite!

Caux
22/8/86
22h55

Hi there!

... I am so excited now I can't wait to go "home" and talk to you. Tonight I spent a wonderful evening with Mr and Mrs Garth Lean and their daughter Mary from Oxford. All three are full-time with MRA and fine Christians ... we started talking about what MRA really is ... (The whole week I tried to find clarity about what I really think, especially as I think you might be critical, that you might think I am naive to speak so positively about certain things.) Mary says much the same as Prof. Marivati[8] yesterday at a meeting of representatives from Africa and Asia: the three basic problems in South Africa are selfishness, fear among whites and bitterness amongst blacks, and that even if Apartheid were abolished structurally,

---

8 Professor in African languages at UNISA, whom I got to know through MRA; currently ANC MP.

people's hearts would have to be changed before peace would truly dawn ... (Mr McKenzie also said that people are so quick to point fingers to other people/countries, especially about political matters, because it does not affect themselves. The moment you start moving on a moral basis and dealing with demands needing to be put to everyone, the rationalisations start following – interesting thought, don't you think?)

... tonight we watched a film on the life of Frank Buchman and his immense love also for the people of Asia and Japan, his respect for and understanding of their religion (although he confessed his Christianity openly and honestly). At one stage I realised with a jolt that I do not really love people of other religions, that their beliefs frighten me or create distance between us; "because they don't believe in Christ". I wondered whether God isn't infinitely bigger than our thinking and theology. I am still working on this problem, but it is as if I am seeing more light (the realisation that we may have much to learn from them, that we shouldn't be so "proud"). What do you think?

The other wonderful experience tonight was meeting Mr and Mrs Bezuidenhout from South Africa. (He is that Mr Timo Bezuidenhout, regional director of Constitutional Development in the Western Cape who often has to deal with squatter problems in the Western Cape, with unrest. He has been on TV often, do you know the one?) Well, he knows my brother Hendrik of the SABC and he is a kindly, open Christian. He is here for next week's industrial section of the Congress – many top businessmen from Japan, the USA and Europe are holding a separate conference to improve links, to discuss MRA's principles – wonderful, don't you think? Mr Bezuidenhout wants to put SA's point, speak against disinvestment and raise money for a low-cost housing project – R500 million!

It came as a gift (surprise) from Heaven to hear from the horse's mouth that the State of Emergency has been quite effective, that black leaders (this I found most important) approached him for help against the violence/intimidation of the ANC, that there has been progress with the National Council. In fact, just seeing that he still has hope, that he knows that we (church, government) have made mistakes needing to be corrected was enough.

As I walked back I had to smile that the Lord let me talk here in Switzerland with someone from SA with hot news from the other side – ten to one it would have been impossible in SA ...

25/8/86
09h17

Good morning!

... I'm sitting in a strange place, on a green bench at Montreux station, waiting for the train to Lausanne, Basel, Utrecht. They are predicting heavy snowfalls tomorrow. To think I'll be back in my little room in Utrecht with all my housemates. Probably Amor and them won't be there anymore, because the church is providing them with a pastorage. (Johan is doing admission exams, they've decided to stay ...) And Rudolf (and his lover) and probably some new faces. I know it's going to be difficult to return and to explain to them all that this week has meant to me. I have realised and seen it all over again that "it is more revolutionary to change people than to liquidate them". (William Nkomo, a founder of the ANC Youth League, said this after meeting MRA – four young whites, after being to Caux, went to him to apologise for treating him (and all blacks) as inferior. This persuaded him to accept an invitation to Caux, where he changed radically and was eventually kicked out of the ANC.) I also saw that what the world and especially SA need are people who think "globally" (who realise that our world is interdependent), who plan regionally (for instance, not to think/work in terms of the preservation of Afrikaner culture and identity, but of the whole of Southern Africa and all its people), who commit themselves personally (in other words, people who are not only honest about the faults of other people and nations, but who are prepared to remove the beam from their own eyes, charity begins at home). People who, in humble submission to God and his charity, devote their lives to combat bitterness, hatred, suspicion between people and nations, to seek God's plan with my life and to live this out in faith.

I have the feeling that I learnt some things this week which are going to make a great difference to the rest of my (our!) life. It's an exciting feeling, but also a bit daunting ...

[The first "big difference" was to write a short letter to a wider audience. The choice of changing my field of study at Oxford was the next, and even bigger difference. This decision was not only the result of the inspiration of Caux, but also a continuing process of political re-education at Maurits Street – this time around with an atheist Afrikaner man as midwife. The uncertainties around these steps now help me to understand why my decision to join the ANC occurred so disturbingly late, how I almost missed one of the biggest changes yet.]

76 Maurits Street
4/9/86

Hello Melanie

I'm making a tape, so I'm not going to write much more now. Please take the enclosed letter about my experiences at Caux to Mother and ask her to type it out to submit it to Die Dinamiek[9] *or perhaps rather* Die Matie[10]. *I even wondered whether one should not submit a shorter version tot* Die Burger[11]/Rapport[12]. *This may be a bit arrogant, because who am I to write to* Die Burger? *On the other hand, I feel these are thoughts which may be of use to someone somewhere – we need "reconciliating ideas" in our beloved country.*

  Why am I so scared of doing something much bigger than anything I've done before? Perhaps because I'm scared of being misunderstood or simply scared of defending a particular point of view in public? What do you think? I have really wondered what to do: one moment I'm so sure, the next all the question marks, uncertainties pop up. Maybe I should do the best I can and leave the rest to you and the Lord, not so?

76 Maurits Street
8/9/86, 19h40

Hello!

I have just come from jogging and had a quick bath, ate some sweet grapes from Greece, put on a tape (Fiddler on the Roof) and now I'm chatting to you. Today was a variable day with variable moods (does this happen to you too? One moment full of life and positive, the next just wanting to lie down and die, feeling we're never going to make it). This afternoon after helping Stewart to the station

---

9 Newspaper of the Stellenbosch Afrikaans Christian Youth Society.
10 Campus newspaper, University of Stellenbosch.
11 Western Cape based, pro-National Party Afrikaans daily.
12 A national (Afrikaner nationalist) Sunday paper.

with his luggage, I returned and started reading the stack of ANC books, magazines and poems left here by Amor and them.

As you can imagine it was deeply disturbing, especially reading about the women and their poems. Also because I will only be able to show you these in a few months (I'll make photocopies). While jogging, I felt sort of scared that all the things I'm seeing and hearing will drive our little worlds apart, and that you would stop understanding me. Then I realised anew that staying close to the Lord would prevent it from happening, although it wouldn't be easy ...

While it was difficult this afternoon looking at the new world of Soweto and freedom fighters (who we so easily call terrorists – before we've listened properly – can you remember the to-do at Stellenbosch when Di Bishop of the PFP referred to ANC people as "freedom fighters"?) I realised again that if I truly believe the Lord to be in control of my life, I must believe it to be His will to come into contact with Amor, Rudolf, but also with Fano and Prof. Marivati; that my surname is and will be "Verwoerd" and that in SA, especially in some circles, this surname bears a negative connotation (which can be positively exploited!).

I just get the feeling that my life may take another direction to the one I planned. Perhaps I won't "just" become a DRC minister in some little village, but maybe in the Mission Church, the DRC in Africa or perhaps not in the Church at all. (I could land up in a body like the Urban Foundation or even in politics!). I don't know. It is just such a curious feeling. We must simply leave it to the Lord and do what is right.

I get the feeling that after hearing everything (this seems to be merely the tip of the iceberg) that has happened recently to Blacks in particular, especially the political system in which my grandfather played such a large role, as well as my Church, that I can't just carry on as usual and forget about everything, reason it away, but that I must give my all under the Lord's guidance to help heal the wounds. Naturally I pray that we do this together, but the Lord must lead you too. I can't expect it from you. I hope it doesn't sound too melodramatic. I hope you understand!

How are things at Crossroads? Are the people still homeless? Can't you organise something to help at the soup kitchens? Whose responsibility is Action Social Justice at the KJA? What is Prof. Willie saying in class, try to find out what he really means ...

Yesterday another chap moved in – Attie van der Merwe (a sociology lecturer *at Unisa). He tells me WP rugby has been doing so well. The rugby-mad SA is really a long way from here!*

Attie is involved in a new institute, the *"SA Institute for Conflict Resolution"*. He offered some useful perspectives from his field, industrial and development sociology (which gave him practical insights into the townships) this evening when we started talking politics.

The most important point to me is that he is radically opposed to Apartheid and that he believes it should change, but that too much attention is given to political change while people naively think that another government will solve all problems. The point is that our country, apart from all the political problems, has a multitude of sociological and economic problems which need and deserve attention. He says we should stop worrying about *"yea"* or *"nay"* to sanctions, or devise political solutions night after night. (This applies to me at Oxford in particular, where all and sundry will want to talk politics with me!)

He also says we should stop being ashamed of our Afrikanerness; we simply are Afrikaners and we should rather start working towards solutions to save what we can.

It is a pleasure to hear someone say: *"Stop maligning the Afrikaner ... rather help to find the solution!"*

Well, it's almost 2 o'clock and tomorrow I want to visit the library. I have new courage for the future – especially because I always want to complicate things and worry and think myself silly.

Rhijnauwen Teehuis
17/9/86
14h05

Hello angel

I'm sitting on the banks of the Kromme Rhijn – one of Utrecht's large canals. Ducks are on the lookout for food between the tables and the sun shines beautifully from between large white clouds. I am looking out over green meadows where cows and sheep are grazing.

Why I am sitting here chatting to you I don't rightly know. It frightens me a little when I think about what I am going to write down, and what I wrote down for the Lord too, during my quiet time this morning after I spoke to you on the telephone.

A few thoughts have become clearer to me lately. Last night Attie came to my room, asking what I was going to swot at Oxford and whether I shouldn't do some or other third-world development study, urbanisation, poverty, sub-economic housing. He believes that there was and is going to be an increasing need in these areas. When he said that, I had to laugh, but it did set me thinking, especially because it touched all sorts of things happening inside me. The clearest of these was my growing doubt whether I would ever be a minister in the white DRC. I have such a feeling that there is "greater need" in other areas, or let's rather say, a need for which I started feeling more responsible and which would be more of a vocation.

This relates to a lot of things: the fact that I am realising more and more that Apartheid is wrong, and worse, always has been; that our people (my grandfather and company) were deaf/blind to those people (the majority) who did not agree with their ideological/theological framework; that our people acted wrongly in the past vis à vis blacks for instance. I know we have done fine things, more than most whites can say ... what I'm really trying to say is that I would like to oppose the terrible effects of Apartheid – perhaps also because my name is Verwoerd, as Professor Marivati said at Caux.

Probably it would be inside the Church, but organisations such as the Urban Foundation and Rural Foundation[13] and their work are becoming increasingly appealing to me. In any case, it doesn't matter so much where I land up, the point is that there are millions of people in our country living under the poverty line, who are homeless. These people need food, clothes, jobs before they can go to church. Naturally this does not exclude spiritual work, but I think that we as a church must be much more involved in poverty which may be the result of unjust structures. (Liberation theology?)

Do you understand the line of my thinking and feelings? The thing which occupies me now, which struck me so suddenly this morning – just like that feeling I had at Betty's Bay that night, when I had the idea to apply for a Rhodes scholarship – is what I should be studying for the next three years. It was as if all the philosophising and rationalising about the existence of God had started looking

---

13 Liberal, private sector funded, development agencies.

like a luxury, given the need in our country. And more so if I still wanted to spend three years after that at the Seminary. It was a feeling of being able to use my time more constructively. If I should follow an academic direction it would be useful to be trained in theology and philosophy, but I doubt it more and more whether this is the course I should, or want to follow.

This is bound to have a profound effect on my (our) life if I should suddenly switch courses (especially during the years at Oxford). I just feel the need to get more practically involved and to stop "philosophising" in my study; to stop being unconcerned about economic and political matters because I "know nothing about it" or am "not interested in it". Naturally I believe that hatred, bitterness (i.e. psychological, theological problems) are just as big or bigger and that one cannot do everything. It is just as if one would be better able to give attention to those problems, to gain more credibility with these people, if one could help them to find a house as well, so to speak.

I don't even know whether it would be possible to change courses or what the alternatives would be, but I have asked the Lord to show me the way and open the doors if He wanted me to do so. You must help me pray too; you are the only person I'm really talking to about this. Because I started thinking about it as a possibility for the first time this morning, and it was almost scary when I realised what was happening. Think how wonderful it would be if we could do it all together – you as the minister/psychologist and me as ..?

76 Maurits Street
18/9/86
13h15

Hi there!

I have just spoken to you on the phone and now afterwards I'm thinking about what we discussed. There were so many things whirling through my head, that I wanted to talk some more ...

Perhaps you will already be able to get practically involved in the suffering and need of people. It was wonderful to hear at the beginning of the first tape (after the snatch of Song Festival[14] – thanks!) how you started feeling frustrated

---

14 Song Festival: annual Stellenbosch University event with many choirs from the different residences participating.

about the same things that I wanted to write to you about yesterday. It is amazing how our feelings correspond and how both of us could (provisionally) study something else, regardless of which direction you choose. I am very excited about the feeling in your heart. It is as if my feelings are confirmed and strengthened by it. There is such great need in our shattered country. Also those feelings you had after Prof. Nico Smith's[15] speech (what a pity you couldn't hear Tutu's speech!) Especially the shocking feeling that in our country of which we have almost always experienced nothing but the best there are so many people who have been deliberately or through circumstances (understandably but not therefore right) deprived of the privileges they would have wanted to enjoy as much as we do. And when they struggled for years to bring about change they were met with violence and lack of understanding and white capitalist selfishness/self-protection.

This must be one of the experiences which shocked and disillusioned me most lately (for which I am thankful), that the world in which most of the inhabitants of our country have been living especially during the past century is so different to our world: so full of pain and rage and frustration.

Last night (or perhaps after I took the decision yesterday afternoon) I finally summoned the courage to finish the book about the police murdering Steve Biko – an unbelievable leader and wonderful human being of whom we don't even know, although it all happened in our country and lives in the hearts of so many. For the first time too the ANC's policy and their violence start making sense to me. I cannot condone it, but I realised with a jolt that ten to one I would have done the same if I had been them (what does this do to military service?).

Don't think I've cracked up. I'm sending you Mandela's speech before the judges during his trial (hope it doesn't get intercepted!). One can criticise it from our little world, but I try to put myself in his shoes, as Jörg Zink quotes an Indian prayer: "Great Spirit, help me never to judge anyone before walking in his mocassins for a month". Quite a shock, and it hurts – there is so much reconciliation and healing work ahead, but what a wonderful challenge, not so? (Especially if we can work together, because of this I am more sure than ever: that I want to work with you in a team, that I cannot and don't want to work without you for a better future for our country, our children. Don't feel threatened, I will ask you ever so nicely and then wait three months for the answer. And if you

---

15 Former professor of theology at Stellenbosch University, who became an outspoken critic of the Dutch Reformed Church's defense of Apartheid.

answer "no" I will kidnap you anyway and give you an injection ... and when you wake up, the ceremony will be over!)

76 Maurits Street
24/09/86
11h20

Hi there!

... sorry if it sounded as if I said you HAD to go and work at Crossroads, it was just a thought. I am glad to hear things are better over there. Thanks for trying to explain to Mother and them that they needn't be so worried ... I just hope my parents understand a bit better after the two rather exhausting letters I wrote them. It was the first time that I really wrote honestly about all those things. It was like a load falling from my shoulders and as if I could be more frank with them in future. I think they feel that way too. I hope it doesn't hurt them or sound too much like a condemnation. Once parents have reached their age and built up such a clear frame of reference, it must be VERY tough when you suddenly hear (and coming from your child in the notorious outside world) such strange noises.

    Yesterday afternoon I worked through the government's publication "Talking with the ANC", which my parents had sent me. For the first time I saw/realised how crass and one-sided the propaganda was; how it is virtually impossible to criticise/recognise their conceptions and conclusions (of selective quotes and without any realisation that they are in turn using ANC propaganda) without "clearly" hearing the other side of the matter. When you come I will show you in several places how subtle, yet how understandable, some of their conclusions are. The more I read, the more I realised how little understanding there is on either side for each other's needs, fears and pain, how politicians/leaders finally just magnify this ignorance by means of their over-simplifications and propaganda (to mobilise/unite their followers). Sigh! I did not really want to write about all this again, but yesterday afternoon I really felt for the first time as if things were becoming slightly clearer to me, as if I could understand the "faults" of both sides. (Sounds as if I know a lot, hey? Hope you understand...)

76 Maurits Street
25/9/86
17h15

Good afternoon!

How are you? I'm not really in the mood for jokes. I've been feeling weak and weedy all afternoon. Lately I have struggled to fall asleep, because all sorts of things (mostly political things, doubts about my future, our future, what to study at Oxford) are whirling through my head all the time. Then I battle to get up in the morning and don't feel rested. I sometimes wish I could stop thinking and just live, but it is tough ...
... hope the photocopies in the letter helped. Especially the one by Allister Sparks about the theological civil war, which I think is a good (tragic!) summary of what's happening in our country. Naturally this is an oversimplification and puts the white churches especially in a bad light. I suppose this is understandable. But I don't really feel like talking politics. Some days I wish I knew how I (and you!) could play our part in this unbelievably complex situation. Then I get so despondent when I look at the extent of the problems and how small and insignificant we are. It really scares me, especially when I think about the responsibility which goes with the huge privilege to gain all those insights and knowledge here over the next few years. What is the Lord going to do with it? Surely He must have a purpose with it. Then it scares me and I wish I hadn't seen and heard all that I have. Dear me!

*I really wanted to chat about this and that but those things/feelings/fears (which I can't fully grasp) are worrying me, especially as my (our) future has changed so rapidly. Sometimes I just want to forget about everything I have written to you and calmly proceed to study philosophy and theology, and forget about the urge to do something practical. I am worried that I might get fed-up after a while, because I'm really interested in philosophy and theology. I'm so used to thinking about myself and my future in those terms. Trusting the Lord is so difficult ...

76 Maurits Street
29/9/86
23h50

Hello my angel!

... I didn't feel so well today. Even jogging did not help, except towards the end when I tried to run and shout all the nonsense and fears about Oxford and my future out of my system.

Lately I have started wondering whether I should try to change direction. Almost as if I were afraid to go working one day among/with blacks (all the danger, conflict, suffering) because how does the Lord protect one? He does not prevent your or my sickness, suffering and dying (or that of our children and families). Sigh! These horrid images and thoughts keep whirling through my head, and I can't get rid of them. Sigh!

After a final conversation with Rudolf and Attie I am feeling better, although with them it still feels as if I'm running up against a wall of negative experiences with the Church and Christians ...

Well, my next letter will come from England. Lately we really have had many conversations this way ...

Lots and lots of love, Wilhelm.

A Sapling in the Wind

A lot had indeed been discussed between early July and the end of September 1986, mostly in a crowded little room at 76 Maurits Street. During this brief period, spent more or less in the same spot, many far-reaching voyages of discovery took place. In due course the seminal effect of this pressure cooker, with all its unplanned and unwanted rebirths, would become clearer.

Instead of viewing my Christian identity in terms of the militaristic image of a "soldier for Jesus", I gradually and cautiously began to feel a growing affinity with trees, although I mostly did not feel like a "tree planted by the waters" (Jeremiah 17).

It was a rather disarmed "soldier" who first walked into the sparsely furnished 4 Thomas Building, Corpus Christi, Oxford, late one night and tired out from travelling (still with a lot of baggage, but more about that later). After three months "abroad" I was armed with the certainty of knowing that there were several things about which I had no certainty at all: what it meant to be "warm" or "cold" or "tepid"; who has to be "spat out"; who is "white", who "black" or "coloured"; who are "Communists" and who "Christians"; how does one fight "for Jesus" – would it be necessary to be like Christ, like the mother pelican on top of the Corpus Christi quadrangle sundial, and be prepared to sacrifice your own blood; who or where is the "corpus" of Christ etc.?

The uncertainty about which academic course to follow for a better understanding of this mundane world was solved mercifully soon. Within a few days after my arrival I was provisionally allowed to register for the versatile PPE (BA Honours in Politics, Philosophy and Economics) in place of the course in philosophy and theology for which I had originally been admitted. So, instead of Christian "principles" the following nine terms (three academic years) were devoted to a relatively unsuccessful attempt at mastering "Principles of Economics", "Economic Organisation", "Political Institutions", "Political Theory", "Political Sociology", "Sub-Saharan African Politics" and "Development Economics".

The humiliating demands of this wholly new academic material, especially economics, a new language of tuition, (Oxford) English and a new teaching method, namely individual tutorials, soon left their mark. In a letter to Melanie on 15 October 1986 it reads:

" ... *recently I have heard little of SA, perhaps because I have stopped watching TV; one so easily forgets everything happening over there. At least it is not the same as the time with Amor and them in the Netherlands. It is incredible to think that if I had not undergone all that, I would in all likelihood not now (and for the next two, three years) be studying economics and politics ...*

The first few terms at Oxford were indeed devoted to discovering why I wasn't really enjoying the "incredible privilege" of studying at one of the foremost universities in the world; in fact, quite the contrary. During this time I tried to keep my head above water academically speaking; to come to terms emotionally with the fogginess, greyness, the cold, shy sun and early nightfall; to keep the long-distance relationship with Melanie (we had got engaged in April 1987) alive; to survive all the culture shocks: it was a strange, relativising experience to look out of my window over that portion of Merton College dating from the 13th century (!), or to write my weekly essays surrounded by books in the Corpus library written long before Jan van Riebeeck planted his momentous foot at the Cape ...

After four terms, at the end of 1987, I gave up for the time being. On 29 December that year Melanie and I were wed at Stellenbosch and I was given leave of absence by Oxford to spend 1988 in South Africa on personal grounds. It was wonderful for a while to climb familiar mountains and to see proper blue sky.

In some of my letters dating from my "first life", the time without Melanie in Oxford, there were some references to a continuing process of political (re)education:

Corpus Christi College
12/2/87, 21h30

Hullo Melanie!

... I enjoyed working on my economics tutorial (first time?), after the lows of the weekend. The last two days I attended two interesting meetings on SA and saw another movie. Yesterday evening (5 pm) I again went to that Anti-Apartheid seminar. It dealt with "resistance" – unfortunately the same speaker. (Apparently he was involved in the 1976 riots and had to flee. Now he is studying philosophy and theology and is a devoted Christian. Just shows you, doesn't it?) In any case, he gave a bit too much attention to the ANC, but it was good to hear that history again and to realise how they were virtually driven to violence by the "regime". This evening I went to a meeting of the Anti-Apartheid student association. (At first I did not want to go, but they were showing a video on the origins of the Freedom Charter, on 26 June 1955. Do you know what it is? I always wanted to learn more about it, so I went.) I am glad I went, because it was an excellent video with interviews, among whom were Oliver Tambo and other ANC members (white and black), which fitted in well with the previous evening's discussions. Now I know that the Government's publication "Talking with the ANC" on the Freedom Charter contains a blatant lie (for instance, they maintain that the document was drawn up by Joe Slovo, a communist).

It is shocking and disturbing to think about: so much sick propaganda which only worsens the conflict and misunderstandings between our people. I wish I could show this video to many, many of our people at home. I saw with my own eyes and heard with my own ears how people came together from all over the country to express their ideals of a free and non-racial SA. That was 30 years ago – how much has happened since then! And at school we hear/learn nothing about all this history! No wonder blacks need "people's education" – the right to hear about their own history in their own schools (which again goes to the other extreme, sigh!).

(It is nice to be able to write these things to you without worrying that you might think I'm mad or misguided.) Then I felt apprehensive about returning to SA. Can you understand it? On the other hand there is such a determination growing in me to get involved and help where I can and where the Lord leads me ...

Corpus Christi
5/3/87, 17h15

Hello there!

... the other evening I had such an unsettling, insightful, sad conversation with an Indian Rhodes scholar from SA (medical student). I just realised anew how incomprehensibly differently people at the receiving end of Apartheid experienced the same country. For instance, not to be able to go where they wanted – and that in your own country! I suppose this is where humour, Christian humour of laughter-with-a-tear is needed, don't you think? Not to laugh away the tears, not to drown the laughter by crying. It is just so difficult to live like this in practice.

On the other hand my "first life" at Oxford shows that I still had many miles to cover before I would lose my fear of a "dirty" direct involvement in the ANC.

Just before my arrival at Corpus Christi the sanctions campaign had built up so much steam that the college's governing body decided (although barely) to close their account at Barclays. New "Corpuscles" were accordingly encouraged not to support that bank. Despite everything that had happened in the Netherlands and despite the moral pressure (or was it because of it – I do have some hard-arsed

55

Boer blood in me, don't I?) I deliberately opened my (modest) account at the Oxford City Branch of Barclays Bank.

In the college I did not participate in many activities during this time. I definitely did not have the confidence to participate in the "house meetings", regular meetings of the JCR (Junior Common Room for college undergraduates) and to speak with all the eloquent, intimidating "rooinekke". Except for one meeting. A decision had to be taken by the JCR whether to send 50 pounds to an ANC school in Tanzania. The motion was put by one of the few "non-white" working-class students at the College.

I must have felt quite strongly about the matter in those days, because I stood up a few times to defend my point. The "me" of then proposed that the money should rather go to organisations inside the country involved in a non-violent struggle against Apartheid. (I can't remember which bodies I suggested.) In the end I could not prevent the money from going to the ANC. An amendment was, however, accepted that the JCR president would write an open letter of support to progressive internal organisations.

Shortly after this I did put the letter's sentiments into action. Although unplanned, I managed to overcome my distaste for party-political involvement for a while. South Africa was again in the throes of a "general" election in 1987. At Stellenbosch a breeze of change had at last started blowing, in the shape of the "Independent Movement" under leadership of Wynand Malan, Dennis Worrall and Esther Lategan. In the Karoo a prominent farmer, Fred Rubidge, also decided to join the "independents". In support of his campaign and to substitute for my friend Hennie Bester, I addressed a political meeting at Richmond. Despite my parents' concerns – they were worried that the media would exploit this "leftist" grandson – I thoroughly enjoyed it. My involvement in leftish, white, mainly Afrikaans politics was cut short by the date stamped on my return air ticket back to England.

Regarding the sanctity of my "soul", the striving for a "pure" heart to be able to "see" God, my first life at Oxford was the gradual start of a long, cold season.

My undigested disillusionment with the DRC led to the fact that neither Melanie nor I, neither in Oxford nor in South Africa, got involved in a particular church or congregation.

Another factor was the emergence of a sceptical awareness of the Church in general. This awareness was increased by my academic exposure to economics, especially development economics. The lonely hours I spent in the cold, modern St Cross building in an attempt to unravel "modernisation vs dependency theories", the "debt crisis", "market failures, government failures and rent-seeking behaviour", "import substitution vs export-led growth models" etc. were not quite in vain. These studies, with my discovery of Charles Elliot's work (especially his book *Comfortable Compassion? – Poverty, Power and the Church*) brought my thinking to an important juncture. I was getting increasingly frustrated with the Church's flawed understanding and actions regarding the large-scale problems of poverty and famine in the world, regarding the unjust power relations between the "first" and "third" worlds. The differences between "charity/aid" and "justice/ development" became increasingly important to me: between the well-meaning handing out of blankets and soup (important, but only providing symptomatic relief or a false sense of comfort) on the one hand, and the development of a "political spirituality" (Elliot) seeking radical, long-term ways of empowering wronged communities, on the other.

In the process a certain alienation from the MRA also occurred, given their (exaggerated) insistence on "absolute principles", on personal morality and individual change. (I still maintained bonds of friendship with individuals inside the movement.)

In the midst of all this alienation from organised Christianity I was still a regular visitor to Christ Church Cathedral, mostly on weekday evenings. The beautiful organ music and singing in the cavernous naves at evensong, the High Church liturgy, focusing on sacraments rather than a sermon, were a balm, a space in which the mystery of God could be rediscovered (occasionally).

This (re)discovery was not limited to the restful silence and beautiful song in an ancient cathedral. In August 1989 Melanie and I undertook a pilgrimage to the Holy Land. This visit to Israel made me even less willing to "sup" (Revelations 3) with that Jesus whom I mostly came across in church services – in white, middle-class Stellenbosch OR in white, middle-class Oxford. In my "noctuary" of that journey I often tried to put into words the contrast between the romantic images of a "gentle Jesus" and the son of the Jewish carpenter in the noisy, dusty heat of Israel. For example:

Ramat Rachel Camping Area, Jerusalem
27/08/89

Jerusalem? What a relativising place, with its many overwhelming traditions, faiths, cultures, smells, colours, foods – footsore old city. Never again will anyone tell me that Christianity must be lived in "beauty" and (Western) "civilisation". Walking through the Old City, especially the Muslim Quarter with its dark, dirty, thronging alleys, it is striking and inspiring to grasp the radical message of Christianity: to love the outcasts/dregs of society IN this dusty, dirty world; blood on the hands of the Good Samaritan!

Back in Oxford
7/9/89

A visit to a holy/unholy land

Greeted by a woman praying at Ben Gurion's bust and a Babel of joy and confusion in the open-air reception area.
   Pita bread and olives in the bustling urbanity of "lowly" Nazreth
   Sunset over the Sea of Galilee, a tent collapsing in an unexpected yet familiar gale, a disco bleating in the campground
   Jerusalem, Jerusalem with her bloodstained 3 000 years "giving witness to hopes and dreams of the diverse children of one God"
   Sabbath in the Jewish Quarter, and an orthodox Jew snoring next to the Wailing Wall
   A siesta in the shade of the Damascus Gate and a "sick" Palestinian who suddenly starts shoving me around – I am told to remove my hat, as he apparently thought I was a Jew. Suddenly I don't feel like a tourist
   Soothed by the pools of Bethesda; we sing the "Our Father", amplified by the unbelievable acoustics of St Anne's
   By luxury "Egged" bus – apparently thanks to German war reparations – to the birthplace of the Prince of Peace, and a salvo of shots as a reminder of a few youths whose search for peace ended last week
   Back to Jerusalem in a rickety Palestinian bus – old, manual gears, blue

number plates, cracked windows, the Jerusalem Post reporting, "... masked youths may now be shot on sight ..."

A visit to the Israel Museum, humbled by the "Shrine of the Book", thousand years of Jewish cultural heritage, and an old man who gives Melanie some cheese biscuits, but is unable to talk about the Germans or "It."

Back again in the "Basilica of Agony", a pro-Catholic sermon and tourists (aided by a priest) taking flashlit photographs

Men in black, the decorated, bearded Patriarch at the head – an incense-shrouded Russian Orthodox procession to Mary's grave

A first visit to the Holy Sepulchre, the hubbub of repair work, of the drills and mini-tractors of the "pigeon sellers"

A second visit, finally a moment of silence at the "Grave of Jesus", and a clumsy priest who (inter alia) shatters a glass bowl

A Sunday afternoon walk up the Mount of Olives, and Palestinian children playing with the insides of a broken tape recorder

A bus trip to Ein Gedi, past Bedouin tents and goats, the world of the Good Samaritan! "The spirit of man is a nomad, his blood bedouin ... and so I came to live my life not by conscious plan or prearranged design but as someone following the flight of a bird" (L van der Post)

Swimming like cork on the Dead Sea, below sea level – which is apparently dying, due to irrigation from the Jordan

A sweaty sunrise on top of Masada – "Masada will not fall again"? Melanie starts arguing with an arrogant "English liberal"

Two days in "Don't worry, be happy Eilat", and a lonely trip through the Negev in an "Egged"bus full of young soldiers, past "firing zones" and burnt-out tanks

Two weeks under canvas in heat and simplicity, a last weekend with (South) Africans in Tel Aviv: air-cooled houses, daily barbecues (home-made sausuage, with skins smuggled in from "home"), an over-familiar DRC service, a video of a second Springbok rugby test ...

Is this the Israel and Palestine
yesterday ... today
the world which God loved and loves,
where Jesus lived (and lives)?

These experiences led to the simple, cautious faith of a David Jenkins (Bishop of Durham) increasingly appealing to me, especially as he insisted that this faith must be lived with the "forced-outs, drop-outs, left-outs" of society:

> *"I simply believe in God*
> *I believe that in the midst of things,*
> *beyond things, behind things and through things*
> *there is a Presence and a Purpose and a Possibility,*
> *who is, basically, infinitely worthwhile*
> *and deeply caring."*
> *(D Jenkins, "Joker in the Pack", 21/5/90)*

Jenkins's faith also fitted in well with all the books, articles and new ideas which Melanie was bringing home. (In 1989 she started an MA in philosophy, a feminist critique of various metaphors/models, especially "Father" and "Mother", used to describe the mystery of God, but more about this later.)

At this stage, where I could identify with the faith of a "joker", the liberation movements in South Africa were unbanned, and Nelson Mandela and others released; Wilmé was on the point of being born, the hourglass of our "second life" at Oxford had almost run out, and the time was almost ripe for joining the ANC. Or so I thought.

After our return to Stellenbosch at the end of July 1990 (I had since then been appointed a lecturer in philosophy), we were determined not to get caught up in the cosy calm and beauty of a white South African middle-class academic's existence. Melanie in particular was very cautious about acting "too hastily", before having informed ourselves about the known-unknown realities of Stellenbosch and the "new South Africa", before knowing about the demands of my new work and especially of a new little person in our home ... not even to talk about the family in my parents' home around the corner. In the end she was the first to join the ANC, while her husband only followed some months later.

These attempts to find our new feet in an old environment in a responsible way, the tension between personal circumstances and the search for ways of giving expression to our new convictions, often left me feeling like "the heath in the desert" (Jer. 17:6). This vacuum of faith explains why the following was one of the few inscriptions in my noctuary of the first year back at Stellenbosch:

24/10/90
The stability of heart

"H Nouwen looked back at his recent life and found how disjointed it was, how it lacked any sort of unity, how the lecturing and travelling ... were all separate and how this encouraged fatigue and exhaustion ... this is the problem of the 'divided heart', of (spiritual) stability as most of us experience it today."

Given the history of my faith it was necessary for this basic lack of direction and its accompanying destructive doubts and guilts to be addressed first before I would find my way forward regarding social and political involvement. "Don't be so worried about whether to join the ANC. First make sure who God is to YOU," was the valuable advice of Barry Grey. It was in his capacity as "spiritual director" during my first "silent retreat" over a rather stormy, wet winter weekend at Vincent Pallotti House. Despite the howling gales and pouring rain, made even worse by the traffic noise of the busy N2 on one side and a large car repair shop (complete with blaring pop music) on the other, this weekend of silence was particularly fruitful.

Pallotti Retreat House
22/6/91

At last I have managed to halt this snowballing absence of silence, to step aside for the first time in almost 12 months back in the country and just before Wilmé's first birthday, and set aside some time to digest my overseas experiences and to attempt to integrate these into my life history.

How nice it is, for the first time in months, to read the Bible again, to write ...

Thanks for Job: I find so much in common with him, in his frustration, struggle and honesty, I found comfort in Your acceptance of his anger, fiery eyes, accusations of a fractured world inside and outside him, in Your rejection of Your representatives, Job's friends, so self-assured about Your image which they bear, so confident in drawing straight lines linking sin and punishment, between chance, injustice and punishment, seeing the relationship between Yourself and Your world and Your people. And then You point to the mystery of Your creation and appear like a riddle in the mirror. And then Job finds peace, although he did not receive answers to his questions.

The last 12 months and ... God?

I fill my days with activities; working, being busy with Wilmé, worrying about our finances.

I feel like a spectator to my own life, with little inner strength to handle crises and the conflict with Melanie. I feel removed from God, but clutch at straws in difficulties: I listen to the King's College choir late at night, I repeat Jenkins's "simple faith" without feeling much, visit various churches ...

Pallotti Retreat House
23/6/91

Dear ... my ... "Caring Presence"

Instead of being a rudderless, anchorless bark on a stormy ocean, I want to be a tree rooted in loving surprises – blown about, waving in the wind, but anchored in the strange rock of a unique, creative relationship with that mystery which at the moment is best explained or demonstrated to me by the words "Caring Presence".

Simple words of a "simple faith" (Jenkins) which sum up the essence of my experience of God overseas and my lack of awareness, especially the last 12 months. A core of being "surprised by love" (starting with people where they are instead of being where I or moral rules want them to be); of a God greater than any one church, tradition, religion; of a Presence in cathedral song and silence; of a Concerned Presence who came and lived in the dusty hell-hole of Israel for a while; of a Caring Presence for the "forced-outs, drop-outs, left-outs" – also for me. When I opened myself to inner healing, in the care of friends, in the mystery of the Church and even now in the care of a mother for our child.

A "Caring Presence" wanting to combine all my unexpected discoveries of people and personal experiences in a warm evening breeze and perhaps wanting to invite me to a creative relationship – a relationship of practical, simple loving which banishes all fear; the fear of reliving, cherishing and exploiting my overseas experiences; the fear of doing my work day after day; fear of debt and finances; fears of people and self-realisation; fear of the future of our country and her people ...

Although I cannot see You, please open my eyes to make me see in my history, the life of our little family, the history of our country, the world, in people and daily experiences, in the Scriptures (in the worlds ahead of, inside and behind the text) and in the Church, your unexpected, Caring Presence!

It would be some time before this relationship of practical love would dispel my fears of the "dirty business" of a liberation movement, before I started seeing the "Caring Presence" even among "terrorists" and "communists".

In this process the caring of a special friend helped dispel some of these fears. We met Graeme MacLean at the end of 1989 as a fellow "Corpuscle", an Australian who had returned to Oxford for a few months to complete a thesis for a doctorate in philosophy. His ability to combine childlike faith with a "tough-minded" schooling in analytical philosophy made him stand out like a sore finger from the sceptical academic world of Oxford. His involvement in our lives (also as devoted "godfather" to our firstborn) was partly responsible for his acceptance of a temporary and then a permanent lectureship in philosophy at the University of the Witwatersrand. After our return he was one of the few people to help us build bridges between the Netherlands, Oxford and Stellenbosch (and is still doing it) on my way towards a God "working, living and loving in the midst of this filthy world"(Zink).

In our many turbulent discussions and holidays spent together, I often experienced his "traditional" certainties as threatening, but it was he, the involved outsider, who again and again stressed the potential importance of the political contribution of this Doubting Thomas (or rather Verwoerd). At the same time he played a central role in cementing in place my rather wavering insights into the priority of a religious or theological dimension in burning issues and choices, inside the family and out.

In September 1991, just after that "stormy" silent retreat, Melanie and I had a brief yet important meeting with President Mandela at Stellenbosch. For her this removed the last remaining obstacle, but for me this meeting just confirmed the potential for pain of my bonds with a particular family and ethnic group or "volk". On the one hand I, like Melanie, wanted to join the ANC; on the other I feared the reaction of the Verwoerd family and the mass media.

Some months later it was a case of eye contact with a friend of Graeme's which helped me to my choice. It was during a conference at Potchefstroom with the theme "Africa Beyond Liberation: Reconciliation, Reformation and Development", from 27 April to 1 May 1992, that Dr Stuart Fowler made certain statements which I experienced as an answer to my question about the mother pelican of Corpus Christi giving of her own blood to feed her child. I had already struggled with this question in my letters from the Netherlands: "How far should one pursue reconciliation? How does solidarity with the oppressed prevent alienation from my own people?" (9/7/86)

In Dr Fowler's paper entitled "Reconciliation in a hetergeneous society", quite a few thoughts hit me between the eyes. In the light of my tendency to dither it was important to be reminded that reconciliation could only take place *"... when people act to bring reconciliation ... If we wait for ideal conditions before acting, we would never act in this world."*

He continued, discussing various requirements for effective reconciliatory action:

Firstly *"critical involvement":*

"We cannot act for reconciliation by standing cheering on the sidelines. We cannot do it from the security of churches and Christian conferences. We must become involved with the life of the world ...

"We will not all be called to be involved in the same way. For some the focus of involvement may be a political party; for others it may be economic life; for others ..."

Secondly, to him reconciliation means *"an overriding commitment to justice".* This implies that in situations where your own community's interests prejudice those of others, *"we must take a stand against the perceived interests of our community".*

Thirdly, he placed great emphasis on practising *"open dialogue", " ... which breaks down the alienating barriers of communal isolation ... it requires of us an eagerness to know our neighbours as fellow humans ... a passionate desire to know our neighbour as a real flesh and blood person ..."*

I remember well how Dr Fowler fixed his gaze on me as he expanded on his fourth prerequisite for reconciliatory action:

Fourthly, empowering action: *"... without economic empowering there can be no reconciliation, yet any effective programme will meet resistance from some of those who stand to lose surplus power. They may become our enemies. Yet the overriding commitment to justice will not allow us to turn back. In this context we remember Jesus' words : 'Do not think that I have come to bring peace to the earth; I have not come to bring peace but the sword. For I have come to set a man against his father, and a daughter against her mother, and a daughter-in-law against her mother-in-law; and one's foes will be members of one's own household' (Matt. 10:34-36).*

"*Here we face both the cost and the limit of reconciliation. Reconciliation requires the redress of power in society. This cannot be done without arousing the hostility from some whose power is lessened in the process. Sometimes these will be those close to us. That is the cost ...*".

Some time after that I tried applying these ideas (hoping to avoid too much moral superiority or hypocrisy). My focus of "critical involvement" was the ANC, because of all political parties it offered the best possibilities of reconciliation, justice and "economic empowerment".

My attempts to "act for reconciliation" as a rather pale sapling with a green, gold and black flag – furled but later flying – in one of its branches, unfortunately meant that shortly after that conference I was being regarded with hostility by many Afrikaners and even became a "traitor" to some people close to me.

But I increasingly wanted to echo the words of Jörg Zink: "Perhaps the heart is only really pure when the hands are no longer afraid of the people's struggle". And when Christians ask me about "the Communists" I tend to concentrate less on economic theories, and rather wonder for how long this word was still going to be misused in South Africa. As a Latin American church leader once remarked: "*When I give money to the poor, they call me a saint; when I ask WHY these people are so poor, they call me a Communist!*"

It was only on the campaign trail during the 1994 elections – and where I sang "Bless Lord, Bless Africa" with the comrades – that I felt spring had come inside me too. Ironically enough this was thanks to "communists" but also to an "un-Christian" professor, Johannes Degenaar. He was one of the few colleagues to offer me moral support in the midst of all the exhausting meetings and (sensation-seeking?) media encounters. He was also concerned about the sordidness of politics and what it could do to one. His wise counsel was to make me listen to a tape-recording of Anthony de Mello, to the surprising, Socratic spirituality of this

Indian Jesuit, and also to Richard Rohr, an American Franciscan and follower of Jung.

During those long trips to and from election meetings in the Northern, Western and Southern Cape, these words of De Mello gained a particular significance for me: *"Go into the heat of battle, but leave your heart at the feet of the Lord"*. It was Rohr in particular who illuminated "the dark, hidden growth" of that winter and the "silent secret" (Van Wyk Louw[16]) of a wounded ego in Oxford and Holland – the importance of failure, of humiliating confrontations with situations and questions to which one has no answers, the resulting uncertainty about "right" or "wrong", "pure" and "soiled", "holiness" and "hypocrisy", about who is a "friend" and who a "foe".

I now want to say with Richard Rohr: *"Perhaps my hands are not so afraid because I am no longer so afraid of my (individual, family, national, Christian) shadows"*. Perhaps because I am no longer so concerned about suppressing my "soiledness" in the name of "salvation" and consequently to project "pollution" onto political **representatives**, especially Communists. Perhaps because I have gradually started breaking down the sometimes unconscious Christian (Western?) "metaphorisation" of colour – perhaps white is not so right and pure, and black not so bad and wrong!

I would now even venture to ask: Isn't God perhaps to be seen in the proud workers on the land, who sing "Nkosi sikelel' iAfrika" with a greasy fist raised; in the eyes of Comrades who don't greet me as their "master"? Is there not a Creative Mystery present in the hundreds of people from Kaya Mandi, who after hearing the election result ran through the streets of Stellenbosch, shouting "Molweni! Molweni![17]" to the cautious White students peering through their windows; in Madiba's embrace of Melanie after her speech in the packed Cape Town Civic Centre to a "rainbow audience"; in the tidal wave of joy for the regained dignity of most people in the country during the election and afterwards? Is there not a "Caring Presence" to be seen in the lack of rancour despite repression as symbolised by some Afrikaners, in the shouts of "Viva" for a Verwoerd inside the ANC?

---

16 NP Van Wyk Louw, one of the foremost of Afrikaner writers and poets of the 1950s and 1960s.
17 "Molweni" "good day!", Xhosa greeting directed at more than one person.

Chapter 3

From white Afrikaner to "pigment-poor" "afrika-ner"

"Why do you Afrikaners try so hard to separate yourselves from us Africans?"
— *Reverend Paul Moyo, Lusaka, 1988*

One night while I was driving an old ANC leader to his house far out to the west of Johannesburg, I propounded to him the well-known theory that if you separate races, you diminish the point at which friction between them may occur and hence ensure good relations. His answer was the essence of simplicity: if you place the races of one country in two camps, said he, and cut off contact between them, those in each camp begin to forget that those in the other are ordinary human beings ... that each experiences joy or sorrow, pride or humiliation for the same reasons. Thereby each becomes suspicious of the other and each eventually fears the other, which is the basis of all racialism.

I believe that no-one could more effectively sum up the South African position today.
  Bram Fischer (Mitchison, 1973:172-3)

If it hadn't been for the Afrikaners, I would probably now have been sitting somewhere in Holland eating a piece of cheese. If it hadn't been for the struggle of the Boers against the English, great-grandfather Wilhelm Johannes Verwoerd would in all likelihood never have packed his bags in 1903 and brought his family from the Netherlands to South Africa to throw in his lot with the Afrikaners. If it had not been for my Afrikanership — or should I say "afrika-nership" — I would in all probability never have joined the ANC in 1992.

What took this Afrikaner into the ANC?

In the light of my family history (to which I will return in due course); given my years as a devoted Voortrekker (Boy Scout) and member of the Rhino team, gaining a Presidential citation (the highest honour in the "Voortrekkers"); given my "struggle for Jesus" from within the white, Afrikaner DRC with white, Afrikaner friends; given my formal education at white, Afrikaner institutions, with Afrikaner Nationalist history as a school subject, it is not surprising that people have started questioning me. Nor that especially some Afrikaners were rather upset to see me on an ANC platform; that some saw me as a "traitor to the volk" and could not understand how I could join a "Black power" organisation wanting to "hand over that for which the Afrikaner had worked and given his blood in battle".

For these reasons I want to tell the tale of a Voortrekker who became an ANC comrade, and a "Rhino" who hunkered down around the same fire with "Young Lions". In the telling I hope to find some clarity about my "treachery" or otherwise. This tale is also part of my search for an answer to this question: why was I so scared for so long of "losing my way" like Bram Fischer or Beyers Naudé? Why was I such a Johnny-come-lately who only started living my political convictions in public in 1992?

Let me begin, as I did in the previous tale, by going back into my own history. This time the spotlight does not fall so much on my personal growth as a Christian, but rather on my development from Afrikaner to afrika-ner, to give due consideration to this important source of my identity.

Where did I as Afrikaner start "losing my way"? Ironically enough I think it was thanks to an Afrikaner nationalist cultural organisation, the Junior Rapportryers. In 1981 when I was 17 it was one of their debating competitions which set the wheels in motion on this important stage of my little Great Trek.

In my first debate, which happened during my last year at Paul Roos Gymnasium, our team had to argue that "The Afrikaner is losing his identity". A devastating sports injury had suddenly given me a lot of time to think about this subject. The books of the "revisionist" historian FA van Jaarsveld, especially *Afrikanerdom under Siege* and *Afrikaner: Quo vadis?* had impressed me greatly. (His view of history would later encourage some "true Afrikaners" in quite another way, namely to "besiege" him with a coat of tar and feathers.) I also remember a conversation with my eldest brother in which I heard to my astonishment his view that "Coloureds" could also be Afrikaners.

At that stage I was still handing out Bibles to "coloured people, whites and Bantoes", which is to say that I accepted the differences between "Whites" and "Bantoes" and the relationship between "White" and Afrikaner quite uncritically. I wasn't totally uncritical about the differences between "whites" and "non-whites" – one of the few entries of a political hue in my English diaries (in place of the usual accounts of the many Voortrekker activities, my sporting feats or my struggle for Jesus) reads:

Friday, 10 March 1978 (Standard 7)

One can call this century and especially the last few years the century of warfare and hatred ...

Now the people will ask, what cause this problems? I think in South Africa, and perhaps in other countries also, the whites got so used that the non-whites do all the dirty work that we are very lazy in a sort of way and that we must realise that they are also people and that we must not look down upon them ... The problem is we are very selfish and I think the main problem is that we misunderstood God's Word and turn it the way we like it.

What actually happened today was that after school our Voortrekker team, the Renosters, went for the final test for our "Burgerpligte-kenteken" (civics badges). After that I went to the Church's bazaar and then to the Voortrekkers ...

All these Voortrekker activities meant that my relations were being complicated somewhat by "Whites" who weren't Afrikaners, that I grew up, in the 60s and 70s, with strong anti-English feelings. My family home and background, in which there was complete identification with the Afrikaner's struggle to be free – first from British imperialism and then from poverty and the English (and Jewish?) "liberal" moneyed interests of the cities – naturally reinforced these feelings. Added to this came the Christian National history at school, with its stress on the development of Afrikaner Nationalism from the Great Trek, the two wars of liberation against the English, the Afrikaner language movements, the battle between the conciliatory politics of Botha and Smuts and the "purified" nationalism of DF Malan, the symbolic recreation of the Great Trek in 1938, the unexpected victory of the HNP (the National Party) in 1948 (with my father telling us how they celebrated in the streets of Stellenbosch), the coming of the Republic in 1961 under the leadership of HF Verwoerd, in the midst of the struggle against rising Black nationalism inside the country and, of course, Communism ...

Possibly even more important were the many storybooks which captured my imagination as a child with their vivid depictions of the unjust suffering of thousands of women and children in British concentration camps, of the heroic yet futile struggle of the few freedom fighters against the might of the "Kakies" and "Rooinekke".

As regards my relations with "non-white, non-Afrikaners" for at least the first two-thirds of my life up to that point, the absence of any clear memories speaks volumes for the "success" of the separation of the races (Bram Fischer[1]). As the wise old ANC leader had predicted to Bram Fischer, my first memory of those days was one of fear: old Jackson, our gardener of many years at Stellenbosch, knocking at our door one Saturday morning, rather shaky on the pins and waving a knobkierie (usually carried for protection against the tsotis (gangsters) of Kaya Mandi, the local township) demanding food. I happened to be alone and slammed the door in his face. Jackson took immediate offence. Unable to gain entry through the front door, he circled the house, shaking his knobkierie, while I watched through a slit in the curtains, sighing with relief when in the end he retired.

My contact with "non-whites" was limited to a few attempts at conversion as a "soldier for Jesus" and a visit to my Uncle Hendrik (Verwoerd) at his mission in Lebowa (before he started his full-time struggle towards realising the dream of an Afrikaner homeland...). Then, of course, there were the people who worked in our kitchen or garden over the years, or those who came asking for work or food. I can't remember any of their names or faces.

But I do remember that my mother would give them food and drink though in special tin plates and mugs (such thick slices of bread with lots of jam, and coffee with milk and heaps of sugar)! No one was sent away empty-handed. In personal relationships, in face-to-face contacts, my family always set an example when it came to (paternalistic) Christian values such as charity, kindness, generosity. From an early age we were taught never to address "the Blacks" by their first names only — my mother clearly remembered getting a hiding when she was a little girl for calling an elderly worker "Jan" instead of by the more respectful title "Outa Jan".

---

1 Prominent Afrikaner who became a member of the SACP and a lawyer defending key ANC leaders during the political trials of the 1950s and early 1960s. He himself was later convicted of treason.

On the one hand I grew up very aware that "us Whites" were different from "the Blacks", that we Afrikaners as a nation could only be free, and remain free, if there was "separate development" for the other "Black peoples". At the same time my parents often said: "You can only expect people of other races to respect you if you respect them..." (Usually followed by: "that's the problem with the coloureds: they aren't a race, and so they have neither self-respect nor respect for others"!) To this day my parents maintain that there's a big difference between "Apartheid" as a system of oppression and White domination, and my grandfather's "national policy" of "separate freedoms", built on "mutual respect and the Christian responsibility" to "uplift them, but also protect their unique cultures". So they also insist "... we are conscious of race, but we definitely aren't racist!", or "... we Afrikaners never wanted to rule others ... Apartheid in its ugly form came straight from British imperialism .. they made a much greater mess in their colonies than we ever did."

That, in a nutshell, was the (black and white) picture I grew up with. It brings me back to my (intellectual) journey away from exclusive Afrikanership, on the Junior Rapportryers' wagon.

In the second round of the 1981 debating competition our team was once more chosen to defend a critical viewpoint. "The Republic Festival should not be maintained in its present form" was the subject this time. We eventually made it to the finals in Pretoria, coming second overall with the scintillating subject "It is not essential for youth to participate in cultural festivals" (!). As a consolation prize I got to shake the hand of the patron, a certain FW de Klerk.

In 1982, my first year at university, I continued this modest foray into nationalist criticism with the JC Smuts Inter-hostel debating competition. This time I had more success in the final round. The judges agreed with us that "The Israeli invasion of Lebanon was NOT justified." For a short while the subject forced me to move outside the white, Christian, Afrikaans world of Stellenbosch. As part of the preparation this former "soldier for Jesus" visited a mosque for the first time. Instead of trying to convert Sheik Abubakar Najaar we asked him to give us some arguments in support of the Palestinian point of view. It was a very strange experience, but it gave me a peek at the world through the eyes of an enemy of the other "chosen people".

In my first year I was also invited by Gys, the leader of our Voortrekker team at school, to a meeting in Cape Town. By candlelight, with the "Oranje, Blanje,

Blou" (national flag) in the background and the Bible in the foreground, and with strangers all round, their faces barely visible, I was solemnly sworn in as a new member of the Ruiterwag, also known as the "Junior Broederbond" – a secret "cultural" organisation aimed at "promoting the interests of the Afrikaner".

Shortly afterwards I joined a "wagpos" (sentry post, local cell) in Stellenbosch. For the next few years I would meet a few friends outside the hostel and go to a professor's house to keep watch over the interests of "the Afrikaners" (in Stellenbosch). (We were always careful never to return together, so sceptical fellow-Wilgenhoffers wouldn't be able to put two and two together ... so our names wouldn't appear in the next sensational exposé, about the Ruiters in the student newspaper.)

At the meetings we spent most of the time talking about the politics of the day or listening to speakers such as Dawie de Villiers, Roelf Meyer or Andries Treurnicht. I can't remember anyone, at least not in my "wagpos", becoming much more active. I was, however, encouraged to oppose the "leftist influences" on *Die Matie*, the student newspaper, by working for the paper. (I did serve as a reporter for a year, although I covered only sports events. After that I started feeling uncomfortable about it and the idea of missionary work in Swaziland or the Eastern Transvaal appealed to me more.)

I didn't always feel at home in the Ruiterwag. From the start I was uncomfortable with all the secrecy and inevitable mistrust from outsiders. I wanted to ask critical questions about "the interests of the Afrikaner". But I decided it would be better to ask these questions within the organisation, together with "the cream of Afrikaner youth at Stellenbosch". It was only in 1987 that I reached the point where I handed in my resignation "for personal reasons". (The most important "personal reason" was called Melanie.)

These hesitant attempts to break away from snow-white Afrikanerdom, from the cosy rut of my student (and Ruiter) life in Stellenbosch, were reflected in an early morning letter to my parents, written at the end of my fourth year at university.

Wilgenhof, 17 October 1985
01.35 am

Dear Mom and Dad

For the last few hours I've been sitting with a few friends chatting about recent events in the country and how each of us has experienced them. I just felt I really wanted to try to explain to you how I see things – with the prayer that I (we?!) won't get too "excited" the minute we start talking about politics, the Afrikaners, confessions of guilt, love of yourself and your nation and your fellow man, etc.

I'm doing this particularly because sometimes (to put it mildly) I get the impression that we talk past one another, that we can't listen to one another with open minds ... It's something I find with so many people, and it's the cause of so many of the problems, bitterness, etc., in this country. It's an experience I've been struggling with for a long time: Why is it like this? What can you do about it? What is the role of the Church? etc.

You can probably put a lot of it down to different backgrounds and experiences, to the infamous "generation gap" ... I've come to believe more and more that the Afrikaner in particular – because of his unique ability to go all out for a cause, his faith in his own capabilities, his conscious striving toward self-determination, etc. – is unable to understand the following words by Van Wyk Louw:

> *Ek haat en ek het lief: ek weet nie hoe nie.*
> *O my land, o my land: jy is ek.*
> *Ek ken jou en ek haat jou, soos ek my haat*
> *Ek het jou lief soos ek my soms lief durf hê.*

> *(I hate and I love: I don't know how.*
> *Oh my land, oh my land: you are me.*
> *I know you and I hate you, as I hate myself*
> *I love you as I sometimes dare to love myself)*

When I read these lines by chance one day, they made a very deep impression on me. They summed up so well what I feel inside, how I am experiencing my Afrikanership: that the contradictory feelings of acceptance and rejection, of pride and shame, of identification and rejection form the two sides of ONE coin. That I can love my people, my history, folksongs and customs, and my language. But precisely because of that I can also feel so bitterly unhappy when I notice faults in the Afrikaner; or when there are people who can't understand how I can be proud of being an Afrikaner; or when my own people (and I) aren't open *enough, or not prepared to admit our mistakes unconditionally or to listen to the (grain of) truth that lies in the words of the critics of our people.*

At one stage I boldly stood up for (only) the positive points of the Afrikaner, Apartheid and the DRC (perhaps especially because there was so much stress on these things in our home). Then I went through a phase where I became very critical of these things. I really didn't feel at home among my own people any more and I even became ashamed of them. (Particularly when I talked to a black man or a PFP [Progressive Federal Party] supporter and was thus confronted with a point of view that wasn't so completely wrong, or as simple as I had always believed.) This probably happens with every young person who's trying to form his own opinions.

In any case, to cut a very long and complicated story short: in the end I came to realise more and more that the attitude I must take is one of loving critic, of loyal opposition. It is just so unbelievably difficult to put it into practice and explain it to people (not least of all myself)!

On this exciting note my eyes are starting to close, so I'll have to complete this at a later stage.

My efforts at "loving criticism" and "loyal opposition" received a boost shortly after I wrote this letter. In December 1985 I got the chance to look at life through the eyes of the "enemies of the Afrikaner people". I joined a group of senior students from the university on a fact-finding mission. The group included a few of the students whose passports had been withdrawn by PW Botha earlier in 1985, among them Hennie Bester. Their offence: they wanted to meet the ANC in Lusaka. With the permission of the University rector and Minister Chris Heunis we were allowed to visit, with as little publicity as possible, UDF and AZAPO members in Durban and Lenasia, Inkatha members in Ulundi and Johannesburg, Percy Qoboza (editor of *City Press*), Dr Nico Smith and youths from Mamelodi, Zach de Beer and other white businessmen (whose passports had not been withdrawn).

In retrospect it is tragic to read in my tour report of the conflict between the UDF and Inkatha in Natal, which even in those days dominated many of our conversations. On the other hand it was an exciting experience for me, as a speaker at a Soweto memorial service in Lenasia on 16 June 1993, to meet some of the young people who had come to speak to us Stellenbosch "boere" back in 1985, so full of mistrust and constantly on the lookout for the security police. This time we were comrades.

But I'm getting ahead of myself. In 1985 I was also rather distrustful of the strapping young representatives of the UDF in Durban and Lenasia:

They set the following "basic demands" (non-negotiables):

(a) The State of Emergency must be lifted and detainees must be released, (b) political prisoners must be released, and (c) the Government must negotiate with all interest groups, including the ANC!

In future they expect the country to become a non-racial democracy (one man, one vote).

A little further on in my report, entitled "A Visit to the other South Africa – in search of a New South Africa!", I had written:

Indians apparently don't share the Afrikaners' fear that the above system will lead to Black domination. It's unclear what the new political/economic system will be like, and, especially, how it will be achieved !! There is, however, no uncertainty about their determination to achieve justice. Children are even ready to sacrifice their education to the "struggle", because it's seen as their only hope!

... The UDF's non-violent methods – boycotts, etc. – lead to violence (according to Inkatha these boycotts are not organised effectively enough). Because of the Government's attitude, the UDF has no alternatives?!

This violence is forcing the government to act, because they have to maintain order and the UDF is actively working to overthrow the system.

This leads again to radicalisation which in turn produces more support for the UDF and allied organisations.

My report also makes it clear that I had more time for Inkatha than the "overly radical" UDF and its "allied organisations" (such as the ANC):

Inkatha's goal is to accommodate both Black and White (with their fears). As someone said:

"Blacks don't want more than what Whites have. We accept that Whites (Afrikaners!) have no other home. We want an Afrikaner to stay an Afrikaner –

ethnicity is a powerful channel of communication (implications for Black-Black conflict?!). But the Afrikaner is not a superior, better child of God. He should not have exclusive political rights, he does not love the country better than I do, he is not my custodian.

"They want to have one citizenship in a single country, but they are prepared to accept a federal compromise. They are in favour of a free market system ..."

What was my conclusion after the "complex, confusing impressions I've gained in the past few days"?

... all groups – particularly Black and White (but also Coloured and Indian) must be released from ideological mindsets. The Afrikaner in particular must realise that Apartheid isn't the only possible system for our country. On the contrary, we will have to realise that Apartheid as a political system has been scuppered by the political realities of our country. That the solution for our problems cannot be found by whites alone and implemented with force (at least, not if we want peace).

The new South Africa will have to be built jointly. The new SA – and the Blacks and people abroad in particular will have to realise this – will however have to accommodate the realities that lead to the policy of separate development in the first place. I think the Black people realise this and respect the fears of the Whites. There is just a tremendous reaction against/repugnance for laws that discriminate on the basis of skin colour.

As in the case of my letters to Melanie from Europe, this report tells a story of expanding consciousness. At the same time the language I used speaks volumes. "The black people", "Coloureds", "Indians", "the Afrikaner", "the Whites", "Us" versus "Them" – these words show that I was still looking at the world through simplistic, racial and ethnic spectacles. My harping on "the fears of the Whites" and statements like "Apartheid has been scuppered by political realities" (i.e. in practice), or "the realities that led to the policy of separate development must be accommodated" showed that in my mind at least, the roots of Apartheid were still alive and well.

But the renaissance of 76 Maurits Street and growing pains at Oxford awaited this rather white seeker of a "new South Africa." From the earlier chronicle about my "Fight for (a Christian Nationalist) Jesus" it is clear that the conclusions I'd reached after my internal fact-finding mission would be thoroughly tested abroad. I quote from a few letters:

76 Maurits Street
14/8/86, 17h30

Hello Melanie!

I have just listened to the last part of your tape and I enjoyed it very much. I feel now like you did then: frustrated and out of sorts. Maybe I've been too excited and happy the last few days. After last night's/this morning's letter I still couldn't sleep and only got up late. It is a really hot, hazy day.

While we were sitting outside eating, Rudolf and Johan started sounding off again about the Afrikaner with his "laager mentality", his inability to learn about other cultures, his immorality when it came to politics, etc., etc. I got really cross and started putting the other side of the argument, but I just couldn't express myself properly in words.

I believe a lot of our soldiers have died in Angola. What happened at the NP Congress? Everything sounds rather mysterious. Johan has also been talking about studies that show the interpretation of history we learned at school – the black men coming down from the North and the white men from the South, etc. isn't quite correct. There was apparently an established black culture at the time in the Cape. Don't you want to check this out for me? An interesting, disturbing thought is also that the Boers were "terrorists" during the Anglo-Boer wars. That General De Wet[2] *developed/discovered guerrilla warfare and that we are now condemning the Blacks for doing precisely what we did. And that they only turned to violence in 1960 (after 50 years of peaceful protest!).*

I know it's not as simple as they make out but through all the talk I hear a little voice saying to me: "What if they're right and I'm wrong?". (Perhaps we're both wrong?!) I asked Gawie to help me yesterday. It's got to the stage where you don't know who to believe any more...Probably all we can do is pray for our country! Sometimes I get a really oppressive feeling when I think about the future and there's no solution in sight. Sometimes I feel as if my head will burst, I'm trying so hard to

---

2 General De Wet: leading figure during the Anglo-Boer War, 1899-1902.

understand it all (perhaps I think too much). What does Prof Willie say?
A month later Attie joined us and helped set my Afrikaner soul at rest. At the same time his voice helped to silence the little voice inside of me.

76 Maurits Street
15/9/86, 01h05

Hello there,

... Attie and I had a lovely long chat. He says we should stop feeling ashamed to be Afrikaners. That's what we are – there's no getting away from it. We should rather start working towards a solution. We must save what can be saved, etc., etc.
It's nice to hear someone say: "Stop slagging Afrikaners off! Rather help work towards the solution!!"

A week later I wrote a "political letter" to my parents in which the different voices within me were given clear expression:

76 Maurits Street
22/9/86 12h30

Hello Parents!

This morning I discovered a few very good (from my perspective!) political/ religious thoughts which made me keen to write the promised "political" letter ...
Certainly politics, and the church and politics, are the areas where we've had the most misunderstandings between us. On the one hand we are very close because I also regard myself as an Afrikaner and I'm proud of it – I think it's an important part of the commandment to "love your neighbour as you love yourself..." (You must remember the letter I wrote, with the quotation from NP van Wyk Louw?) That brings me to the other side, where I think our worlds are very far apart ... Especially considering our different experiences, not only in South Africa, but especially in the last two months with Amor and the others, as well as in Switzerland.

Caux definitely made the greatest impression as a result of the open, loving manner in which I gained insight into the lives of my fellow South Africans in particular. Blacks and Coloureds who are also people just like me. People who also love their language, their culture and their country. People who also fall in love and have families, who have feelings like us whites, BUT who have been on the receiving end of Apartheid for all these years. Apartheid with its pass laws, group areas, forced removals, restricted facilities, theatres and beaches – even if you're a highly educated, civilised Black man; the homeland policy (the homelands making up 13 percent of the country), with no property rights outside the homelands (even if your family has lived there for generations and you view Soweto, for example, as your home town); no right to vote – no say in the political policies that control your life. These people also have a different view of history, for example White exploitation of cheap black labour since the colonial period, and still in the mines. And then there are the White and Non-White signs all over the place. "Non-White" – in other words I am not a Black man in my own right, but a NON-White; White is the standard by which humanity is measured.

These are just a few of the opinions held by the people I've met. (I wish you could also have contact, real contact with a black man or woman – on the level of friendship and not the level of boss and underling!)

You can of course respond to many of these accusations by saying: "but that isn't what we intended"; "but just take a look at the situation in the rest of Africa"; "look what we've done for the Blacks over the years (and now they are burning their schools down again!)"; "this country was built with White money and skill"; "we have to contend with troublemakers and communist agitators", etc., etc.

Naturally many of the arguments are true (from our perspective, anyway). There are understandable reasons why Whites, and we Afrikaners in particular, insist on self-determination and the maintenance of self-government, as well as for our fears of Black domination, Communist "total onslaught", etc., etc. It gets even more problematic when you consider what the alternatives to Separate Development were or what type of political system could accommodate our unique ethnic composition as well as a healthy economy.

Oh well, I don't have a good answer for the last question, in particular. What is clear to me, though, is that Apartheid, or any political system worked out only by white politicians – even if they genuinely believe it's the best solution and they're acting according to Christian principles – will never work. Such a setup is in any case demeaning to the majority of our fellow South Africans. It is becoming clearer and clearer to me that we must move away from a political policy (and ideologies) that are based on people's skin colour (which unfortunately in South Africa coincides to a great extent with a person's level of education, social and economic standards). Sure, in this process Whites will have fewer privileges and fewer beaches, but we stand to gain in human relations, cultural interaction and enrichment and Christian charity, and we will be able to look forward to a more peaceful, just and human future for the majority of people in our beloved country. A country for which our forefathers – just like the Blacks now – fought the Blacks and especially the English and used tremendous force against their oppressors.

... All these things have made me think I should "philosophise" less and get practically involved, considering the need in our country, particularly among the blacks, but also when it comes to relationships between Black and White. I'll just have to deal with the implications of this for my studies at Oxford (and my future), when they arise. (I won't take any hasty decisions, OK? Don't Worry!)

Shortly after my arrival at Corpus Christi I received a letter from my father in which he expressed his concern about my "development". Besides well-meaning advice and warnings about previous grandsons of "famous granddads" who landed up "on the wrong side", such as Colin Steyn[3] and Bram Fischer, he attached a copy of a letter to a newspaper by my uncle, Professor Carel Boshoff. "Whites in a crisis of morality." (In the letter he rebuked Dr Anton Rupert[4] for mentioning a Boshoff and a Tutu in the same breath.) (*Die Patriot* – Conservative Party newspaper, 10 October 1986.)

These letters gave me the chance to try to put into words the crisis my Afrikaner identity was going through, and to try to draw the outline of a new identity for the years ahead. At the same time it is disturbing to see – in spite of my experiences in Holland, in particular! – how I could still make the statement that "separate development ... makes political/moral sense but not economic sense."

---

3 Grandson of MT Steyn, former president of the Orange Free State Republic.
4 Leading Afrikaner business man and advocate of reforms from within the National Party since the 1960s.

Corpus Christi College
28 October 1986

Dear Mom and Dad (and Uncle Carel)
The most important thing I want to say with reference to Dad and Uncle Carel's letters – it really hit me like a hammer blow when I realised the possibilities of constructive co-operation – is that we agree on an awful lot of things. Perhaps because, not so long ago, I won a debate defending the motion: "The idea of a White homeland is justified".

But, seriously: we more or less agree when it comes to an analysis of the current situation, the historical causes, and I find that really wonderful – I believe it will make us more open to understanding one another's differences. We also share the same goal – the reconciliation of interests, peace, progress and security! We share the belief in the right of the Afrikaner people to maintain their existence as a nation and we especially recognise the sacrifices this nation had to make in order to achieve that independence. I could go on in this vein ...

I want to be so bold as to suggest something – particularly in view of some of the things Uncle Carel said in his letter: "the stability and prosperity of the last half-century have been built on a false reality" and "... became part of the liberation struggle of the blacks". When one manages to get past the emotionality and anger and the betrayals, it's very similar to what the Blacks are saying, and what they are trying to change in their liberation struggle. After all, they are rebelling against à "false reality" that doesn't give them "the best of both worlds" (Uncle Carel), which is built on their labour without really enabling them to enjoy the fruits of that labour (on the contrary!), in which they are "dominated" by a minority.

Since the formation of the ANC in 1912 they have tried to get the message across to Whites: Please don't prescribe what's best for us! We don't agree with the policy you developed; we don't feel or experience the good intentions behind it in reality, etc., etc.

I don't want to carry on too much in this vein. I'm just trying to say: if we really listen and get past "Marxist analyses" in the Kairos document [5], Belhar confession (Mandela's speech during his trial), etc., then it's just people with broken hearts rebelling against an "immoral, intolerable" (literally) (for them) system.

Yes, I know this is an oversimplification and I've made them sound like angels,

---

5 A watershed confessional document adopted by the Dutch Reformed Mission (coloured) Church in the early 1980s condemning Apartheid as a heresy, calling on the white mother church to repent and reject their defence of Apartheid.

but what Uncle Carel said in his unbelievable critical analysis of the current order gave me the courage to say it.

Besides, I'm unclear about the use of the words "Whites" and "Afrikaners". Are the Afrikaners among the Whites who built the "false reality" over the past 50 years? Are the Afrikaners among the Whites who prescribed to the Blacks for all these years (from Christian, paternalistic motivations?), what was best for them, who enjoyed the "stability" and "prosperity" at the expense (literally) of the Black people?

If this is in fact the case, then it has far-reaching implications for our "right" to maintain independence at all costs. Without saying the other party is guilty, don't we as a nation, as Whites, bear the guilt for the "judgment of history" (Uncle Carel) which our country is presently facing? Isn't it terribly important, before we go on to work for a "hopeful future", to admit our guilt and ask for forgiveness?

Let me put it this way: as important as Dad's political proposal is the attention to hard work (with costly sacrifices – perhaps in terms of our self-esteem?) to shattered human relations – after all, we want to "reconcile interests", and "establish good relations with other nations" (Uncle Carel).

So, basically I'm just trying to emphasise the implications of Uncle Carel's critique, our critique of the current state of society. Not only the implications for the future "free, safe volkstaat", but also for the ways in which we will reach this goal, for the past and our share in it, for our daily behaviour, for our judgment of the "black liberation struggle". Isn't the struggle of the Afrikaner essentially the same as that of the Black man? Naturally there are various solutions/visions of the future, etc. But aren't they both fighting against the same thing – the immoral, futile, selfish struggle of Whites who wish to maintain Apartheid in a common country (to use Oom Carel's description). Isn't it one of the greatest tragedies of our land that Afrikaners and Blacks are fighting one another? I'm sorry to harp on this point for so long – it just makes me so terribly sad, on the one hand, and yet hopeful and excited on the other hand. I hope the rest will be a bit briefer – there are so many things I'd like to say!

As far as the "inevitable eradication of whites in a unitary state" is concerned: Is this necessarily a foregone conclusion? No Black man I've ever spoken to wanted to shut out the Whites. They only want to be accepted as equal partners, as fellow South Africans (they also have a great love for the country ... "ons vir jou Suid-Afrika" also lives in their hearts!!). Are the only two alternatives those that Uncle Carel discussed? Isn't THAT perhaps an oversimplification? – White versus Black, while both White and Black consist of differing interest groups. Naturally minority rights must be entrenched and protected in one or other form of federal system ... Even more important: we must work it out TOGETHER. And for us as Whites it will be very difficult and take a lot of patience, faith and sacrifice.

This brings me to the "vrye volkstaat"(free, white Afrikaner homeland) alternative:

How many Afrikaners (especially in urban areas) and how many Black people (particularly the younger, future generation) regard themselves as part of a "volk"? How many Black people really support the Homeland policy; how will they be persuaded peacefully to follow an example with which they have so many negative associations? (something unique to our country, I believe).

My most important problem with the "vrye volkstaat" idea and what I think is the main cause of the failure of separate development, is that I don't think the Whites were simply "talked out" of the policy of "separate freedoms" (freedom as defined by the whites, and interpreted from our point of view).

No, perhaps the price was literally too high. In other words, in terms of political principles, etc., the policy made sense (also in terms of the Christian recognition of equality and diversity before God and the most just system in which both of these principles could be applied), but not in terms of economic principles...

I could go on like this, I hope I don't sound too critical. Sorry about the writing, it's getting really late...

A few months later, on a visit to South Africa for the Easter holiday in 1987, I got the unexpected opportunity to put forward the above political views in public for the first time. I have already referred to my small contribution to Wynand Malan and co.'s "Independent Movement", which blew like a fresh breeze through the musty room of yet another white "general election". It even blew to the isolated farming community of Richmond. My speech on this occasion gives an idea of my views at the time on political parties and the ANC:

Ladies and Gentlemen

Thank you for giving me the unexpected privilege of allowing me to participate in the work of the Independent Movement ... I'm standing here not as a political leader or as someone who knows the problems of this community particularly well ... I am a student at Stellenbosch University who's proud of being Afrikaans, who loves this country, South Africa, and who has a lot of respect for the farming community ...

I want to say to you tonight: I'm tired of exhaustion and despondency. I'm tired of the dark pictures being painted of the future. I'm terribly worried about many of our young people who are joining the Great Trek abroad – to Australia, England, the USA, but also to Zambia and Tanzania and the ANC. I am sick and tired of cynicism, of people who say the only thing for Afrikaners to do is to form a laager and fight to the death.

I have lost my faith in the established political parties.

The NP is at a dead-end, without credibility, with defective, shortsighted leadership. Since last April (1986) reform has been quashed and replaced with raids into neighbouring states (among other things). In Stellenbosch they are the "great reformers", but in the countryside the NP posters declare "separate schools, separate suburbs"!

The Conservative Party is stubbornly and blindly looking for solutions in a manner that didn't work 20 years ago and fills the majority of people in the country with revulsion.

The PFP people sound terribly liberal, enlightened and so on from their lovely suburbs in Cape Town and Johannesburg. But when the crunch comes, when courage and sacrifice are called for, they vanish like mist in the morning sun.

The Independent Movement focuses on the values that the various groups share instead of a new political model that will simply increase the level of conflict ...

This movement fills me with hope: instead of just looking north and seeing "Swart gevaar[6]*", "the rest of Africa", and "Communism", they also look to the south, where two mighty oceans meet and nurture a rich sea life. Now don't get me wrong, I'm also against Communism, but it's just as naive to look for a Communist behind every bush as it is to deny the reality of Communism.*

---

6 Literally "black peril" – a very effective slogan in white SA, referring to the perceived threats posed to white "civilisation" and especially Afrikaner interests by the "large majority" of Africans in South Africa and "the rest of Africa".

As far as the ANC is concerned:

We must simply accept that the ANC is there. It has the support of many Black people and cannot be wished away. It also can't be shot away, because then its support will just get greater – they say that every time Adriaan Vlok[7] appears on TV another 500 young people join the ANC! The only alternative is to talk. There is propaganda on both sides, but the ANC is more than just a bunch of armed terrorists. It is the symbol of the black man's struggle ...

I want to conclude with the words of Paul Kruger: "Take that which is good from the past and build the future on it." I beg you not to make the same mistakes as in the past, to ask forgiveness for these mistakes, to take pride in the good things and to build the future with self-respect, courage and INDEPENDENT thinking.

In terms of this young "boer's" own personal "Great Trek" it's interesting to see how I was still describing myself as an Afrikaner with a capital A. As far as political parties were concerned, I'd moved away from the mainstream "established parties". But I still saw my options as limited to white politics. Why?

What hindered me when it came to daring political choices was the fact that I belonged to a certain rather prominent family, I was stubbornly loyal to the Afrikaans people and I was devout in my DRC beliefs. My struggle to find out what it meant to "build the future with INDEPENDENT THINKING" in view of my background, was reflected by a stormy diary entry about the Day of the Vow[8] in 1987. This day was very important to me as a Voortrekker at school. Our Rhino team regularly handed out programmes at the annual commemoration service in Jonkershoek. But in 1987 I really didn't know what to make of an invitation from my parents to accompany them to a "proper Day of the Vow celebration" of (conservative) "true Afrikaners".

16/12/87
01h26

... Lord, I'm in a turmoil about the Day of the Vow again. Suddenly everything seems so confused. The whole story of December 16 just doesn't fit in with my concept of God. Were the Voortrekkers at the Battle of Blood River just a bunch of fanatics who "bribed" God to get them out of trouble? Or did You help Your

---

7 Minister of Law and Order at that time.
8 An Afrikaner Nationalist public holiday on 16 December commemorating a "Godgiven" victory of Voortrekkers in 1838 against a large number of Zulu warriors in Natal, also known as the Battle of Blood River.

children in need – not because they were white or because they were a "chosen race"? But then what of the defeat in the Second Anglo-Boer War, and what about all the Afrikaners who died in the two World Wars? What about the WHOLE picture of those events? (What about the Zulu children who were apparently kidnapped by the Voortrekkers?) Does a nation have the right to make a vow and force it on succeeding generations? What about my relationship with the family and with the "volk", to whom the Day of the Vow is such a precious day, integral to what it means to be an Afrikaner (for quite understandable reasons)? Should I go to Goodwood with my parents and Melanie tomorrow (actually later today)? It doesn't feel to me like the right thing to do. Considering my present convictions, isn't it too great a compromise? I don't understand Your involvement in the history of the Afrikaners, and the Zulus, and in South Africa's past ? Oh Lord, I don't know, I DON'T KNOW! I don't know about the Day of the Vow. I don't know what my role is in this country. I don't know how to handle the relationships with my family (near AND far) and with Melanie...*

All this angst makes me sick! But what the hell should I do? Perhaps I should listen more to You: "My grace is enough for YOU..." ...I want to draw a line through the last sentence – NO!

This struggle in the early morning hours with a rather invisible God and the spirits of my forefathers helped me understand why it would take a good few more months before I went further than simply pleading for dialogue with the ANC from a safe, white political platform. I'd progressed from mere verbal criticism – in a letter to Melanie about the NP's propaganda pamphlet "Talking with the ANC". In 1988 I got the chance, along with a few Stellenbosch students and lecturers, to "pollute" my ears by going and listening to the "truth" – this time at first hand, in Lusaka, Zambia. (I was too afraid to try for a place on the historic 1987 trip to Dakar ... "what if they withdrew my passport ... what about my studies in Oxford? What about my family?" etc., etc?)

So in June 1988 I took my first trip to "darkest Africa", to the "rest of Africa" north of the Limpopo – a far cry from my usual holiday trips to the south, to the snow-white beaches of Betty's Bay. At the age of 24 I danced with a number of richly pigmented "brothers" for the first time – on the upper deck of the *Mtengere* (tired, overloaded and about to embark on her umpteenth journey on Lake

Malawi). I even sang along with my fellow dancers to the chorus of the blaring reggae tune: "Back to our roots ..." ! After three weeks in Malawi, Zambia and Zimbabwe it was, however, no longer so clear what "back to our roots" meant. But the sojourn in black Africa was very important in my quest for an answer to the question posed by the minister of the Reformed Church of Zambia whom I met in Lusaka:

"Why do you Afrikaners try so hard to separate yourselves from us Africans?"

Shortly before our departure I'd formulated this question in my diary:

*Irony of my "volk" and my language: we are called **Afrikaners**, which means we are of Africa, and our language is called **Afrikaans**, an African language. Yet we have so little understanding/love for Africa and its people. We share the love of the soil, spiritual sensitivity, love for people (to a lesser extent), etc. And yet there is so much misunderstanding, fear, hate in South **Africa**.*

Bless us today Oh Lord ...

This minister's question formed the theme of my tour report, a milestone in my trek through the "world within". It was an important question, an exasperating irony, a difficult challenge.

Some of the entries I made clearly show my progress towards developing a more inclusive understanding of what it meant to be an Afrikaner:

*"... **As an Afrikaner I regard myself as an African, my roots and my mother tongue are firmly embedded in Africa, this is where I see my future** (emphasis added 1994). This conviction was strengthened by the moving way in which we were welcomed as Afrikaners by fellow-**Africans** in the countries we visited...*

Afrikaners are not "chosen" to separate themselves, but are in a unique position – given our history of oppression by colonial powers, our understanding of the effects of urbanization on rural people, our European heritage, our love for the land and love for people – to bridge the differences between African and Western values/cultures, between traditional and modern Africa."

At the same time the book that formed the basis of most of the conversations we had during the study tour: *The Option for an Inclusive Democracy. A theological-*

ethical study for appropriate social values for South Africa, helped me judge not only the practice of Apartheid. In contrast with, for example, my letter to my father and Uncle Carel in 1986, I would henceforth regard the **theory** and **theology** underlying "Separate Development" a lot more critically. The following quote might sound a little too theoretical, but considering my background as a philosophy and theology student, it shows what an important barrier in my mind had to be broken down:

Let me begin this section by saying something about the central theme of "unity and diversity", about the reasons behind choosing an "inclusive" democracy. Many people outside South Africa found it strange and dangerous that we placed so much emphasis on "diversity". The next edition of the booklet must make it clearer that our target-group (as I understand it) is primarily white South Africans coming from a Reformed church tradition.

This is a group of people who have been indoctrinated by an ideology and a theology of Apartheid. Many of them believe that people are created equal before God and are equally sinful, they believe in the transcendent unity of the Church of Christ. At the same time so much importance is attached to differences in terms of race, culture, language, etc., that the manifestation of this equality and unity in church structures and political, economic and social integration, would inevitably result, they believe, in conflict: the dominance of the black majority, the destruction of each group's "God-given right to self-determination."

Thus the differences become divisive, leading to compartmentalised values and conflicts between preaching and practice, to so much dehumanising racism in a country where 78% of the population confess the Christian faith. Apartheid effectively separated people, but destroyed unity and equality at the same time. With the current ideology of the "total onslaught" this process is continued.

That is why the approach of this booklet is so important. It attempts to formulate alternative theological-ethical guidelines in which the emphasis shifts from differences to unity. This is done by showing that from within the Reformed tradition diversity must be regarded positively, as the prerequisite for unity. Outsiders might regard this as a platitude. Actually it is a call for a reformation of Apartheid theology's distortions of the Protestant tradition ...

"Viva Verwoerd!", 13 May 1993 - *acknowledging those unexpected, deeply moving Vivas after my first appearance on an ANC platform in the Parow Civic Centre.*

May 1964 - *with my mother, Elize (neé Smit), and my father, Wilhelm Johannes Verwoerd.*

31 May 1986 -
my three brothers and I, Gideon, Dirk, Hendrik (in the usual order).

8 September 1964 - *on Oupa Hendrik's lap with Ouma Betsie and the other grandchildren, celebrating his 63rd birthday at Libertas, Pretoria.*

1978 - *our disciplined Voortrekker team, the "Rhinos". From left to right: Francois Smit, Dreyer Lötter, Gys Wessels, Gabriël Kroes, Hendrik Lemmer and Johan Hattingh.*

1980, Coetzenburg - *on my way to that (unfulfilled) dream of becoming a Springbok middle distance athlete.*

March 1986 - *I received the BA Honours degree in Philosophy from Prof. Mike de Vries, then Rector of the University of Stellenbosch.*

October 1986 - *in full academic attire after being accepted formally at the University of Oxford, standing next to the pelican sundial in the quad of my college, Corpus Christi.*

November 1986 - *I am struggling, third from the right, to keep up with the pace in the Christ Church Regatta.*

29 December 1987 - *I got married to Melanie Fourie.*

2 July 1988 - *in front of the Pamodzi Hotel, Lusaka, during my first journey "into the rest of Africa". From left to right: Johann Kinghorn, Hennie Kotze, Johan Groenewald, Braam Olivier, Jacques du Plessis, Hein Brandt, Martin Pauw, Cornis van der Lugt, Daan Mostert.*

May 1990, Oxford - *the morning before the start of the dreaded "Finals", the only examination after three years of "reading" for my degree in Philosophy, Politics and Economics.*

March 1991 - *our daughter Wilmé contributes her "yes" to the last "whites only" referendum on the continuation of negotiations by the De Klerk government.*

28 September 1991, Stellenbosch - *at last I got the chance personally to convey my deep sense of sorrow about the injustices of Apartheid to Mr Mandela.*

December 1992, Stellenbosch - *after the baptism of our son, Wian Brandt Verwoerd, at the home of my in-laws. Back row: Oupa Jan Brandt (Melanie's maternal grandfather), my mother Elize Verwoerd, Melanie holding Wian, my father Wilhelm Verwoerd, my sister-in-law Melissa Fourie, my mother-in-law Lenie Fourie, Nadine Fourie (Melanie's other sister). Front row: Ouma Lenie Brandt, Wilmé, "Outan" Rust (my maternal grandmother's sister), Ouma Charlotte Fourie.*

16 June 1993, Lenasia, Johannesburg - *singing Nkosi Sikelel' i Afrika after a Soweto Day memorial service.*

1995, Paradyskloof, Stellenbosch - Wian and Wilmé with Graeme MacLean, Wilmé's godfather.

February 1994 - *with Melanie after the "Never Again" rally outside the gates of the Victor Verster Prison, in the run-up to the General Election.*

10 May 1994 - *a few comrades celebrating President Mandela's Inauguration at the Union Buildings, Pretoria.*

An afrika-ner in the ANC?

Why did another four years elapse before my resistance to dehumanising Apartheid and an illegitimate government, and my commitment to a non-racial inclusive democracy, lead me to throw in my political lot with the ANC?

Part of the answer has to do with the difference between a "pro-South African, pro-African Afrikaner" (as I described myself after the tour) and an "afrika-ner" member of the ANC.

Since discussions with ANC members in Lusaka weren't part of our official programme at that dark stage of the "total onslaught" I couldn't report on them. My diary, however, contains several critical impressions of the ANC, based on long discussions in the Pamodzi Hotel, Lusaka.

We were met at the airport by Steve Tshwete[9], greeted in Afrikaans and quizzed about the state of Western Province rugby ... not quite what I expected from a "terrorist leader" at all. The ANC's National Executive Committee happened to be having a meeting at the time. This gave us the chance to shake the hands of quite a few notorious people, even the "arch enemy" Joe Slovo. I felt like a traitor.

Of course I have to talk to the ANC, but to shake their hands as if we are all big buddies ... I don't feel so good about this. ... Here I am shaking the hands of an MK leader and a Communist when a few months ago my brother risked his life to go and fight somewhere in Angola ... What about all the chaps who lost their lives in the struggle against the ANC?

After these emotional handshakes we spent a Friday afternoon and a Saturday listening to some of the younger "comrades" giving their interpretation of our country and the ANC's history, the justification for the "armed struggle", the road ahead. Thabo Mbeki joined us on the Saturday afternoon to listen to "our side" of the argument and answer questions.

Friday Night, 1 July 1988
Lusaka

This afternoon in the Pamodzi – mixed feelings! It seems to me I'm a very emo-

---
9 Prominent ANC activist, currently Minister of Sport.

tional person. That's important, but also dangerous. I must share my feelings with other people, because it brings me down to earth a bit:
- *to me there's a big difference between being pro-ANC and pro-South Africa. The ANC is certainly an important part of the solution, but it isn't THE solution. To me certain individuals within the organisation are quite acceptable.*
- *I am amazed that they have so little information about what is going on in rightwing Afrikaans organisations at the moment!*
- *I feel comfortable about the ideal of a democratic South Africa. It means that these people must also be part of it.*
- *on a secular level I believe the "middle ground" is important, but this underlines the difficult position/dilemma of a bridge builder. Now this experience is more on a personal level, but later in my life it may be important when I start building a new South Africa, etc.*
- *on a spiritual level: Lord, I want to believe that what I'm doing comes from religious conviction, hate of violence, of sin, in the service of reconciliation, peace between peoples and with God. In other words, it's my little part in bringing about Your kingdom here on earth ...*

Rev Paul Moyo yesterday: the irony of South Africa's struggle against communism in the name of God – it turns black people both inside and outside South Africa into communists, whereas by nature black people are opposed to an atheistic communism. They are definitely in favour of African socialism, though...

Sunday 3 July 1988
Lusaka

The past two days have been incredibly interesting, disturbing and enriching. Important observations:
- *"transference of power to the people" is important, but who are these "people"?? Sometimes it's everyone who stands for a non-racial democracy. At its deepest, however, the "mass revolutionary base" is "Black". In other words when it comes to strategy the black power base within South Africa is the controlling factor.*
- *NP/ANC: Basically they have the same nationalism, megalomania, origins ... they make decisions on behalf of others and are thus characterised by limited*

democracy. I agree with the group member who said: "The sooner we get rid of both the NP and the ANC the better."
- Johann Kinghorn's description of the dilemma we find ourselves in: we share with the ANC the ideal of a non-racial/inclusive democracy, but what we're doing, the bridges we are trying to build, weakens their power base, and what they're doing with their armed struggle against Apartheid reduces our credibility in the community we come from.

Black "liberators" certainly have a constituency, they are heroes in the community, etc. Even people like Beyers Naudé owe loyalty to one group. In a certain sense it's easier than my/our problem of "being alone" (perhaps another form of struggle/sacrifice, even though I'm not suffering financially, etc.): we are trying to bring about reconciliation; we are identified with our people, but are critical of their solutions; we do not share the ideals of many Afrikaners, yet our membership of this community places limitations on the strategy we're following – that's why we oppose the "armed struggle". There is a contradiction between "revolution" and "negotiation"!
- are non-democratic methods really the only way to a true democracy?!
- the ANC is certainly a liberation movement, but it doesn't seem as if they have much clarity about what must happen after liberation.
- their support for socialism is a big problem, but it can't be shot away – quite the opposite!

Part of the reason why it took so long for a wagging finger of criticism to become a (singing) fist in the air had less to do with my questions about the ANC than with some of the words I used far too readily in my tour report. The problem was still the capital letter of my "Afrikanership".

The evaluation of the tour is contained in the foregoing impressions and comments. This often painful experience was of great personal value to me. In no other way could I have experienced on an existential level that **as an Afrikaner** I am part of **Africa**, that **my people** have a lot to learn and a lot to give ...

After three weeks "in Africa" (well, in a few areas of three countries in southern Africa, to be precise), I was certainly far more aware of the failed marriage between Afrikaners and Apartheid. But I was still a child of that marriage, my consciousness was still barricaded with words born out of "separate development": I still spoke of "my people", I still thought of myself as "an Afrikaner", I still dreamed of "Africa" versus "the West". As someone quite correctly noted: *"You are not a country, Africa, you are a concept, which we all fashion in our minds, each to each, to hide our separate years, to dream our separate dreams".*

My diary of 1988, the year Melanie and I spent in Stellenbosch, tells of my attempts to overcome "separate dreams" within and outside myself.

Stellenbosch
11 November 1988

Last night in my college room I listened again to the tape of Larry Ellis's speech {Larry is an African-American student, a friend who in 1987 was doing postgraduate studies about the relevance of Gandhi's philosophy to resistance in South Africa.}
   "Militant non-violence" as "truth-force", "soul-force" to make people "visible" and "valuable".
   The ways in which society is structured, the norms that determine people's "visibility" – wealth, race, family, etc. – make certain groups (internationally) "invisible". The consequences of this are "soul-crippling", dehumanising.
   Larry also makes an interesting distinction between two types of oppression:
- *"instrumental oppression": "denying some people access to a society's resources", as in SA*
- *"expressive oppression": indirect, unofficial oppression (attitudes, character assassination etc.) which is worse than "instrumental oppression", because it breaks people's spirit, is harder to identify and so difficult to combat...*
   It's actually unbelievable how invisible the majority of our country's population is to the Whites in particular – Apartheid on TV, in the newspapers, in our daily lives. Whites see only low-class workers/the unemployed and "Police File" on TV.
   What the Conservative Party (Andries Treurnicht last night on TV) has to say about this is tragically ironic: "If you share powers with the Blacks you end up

with nothing in the long run ..." So, hold on to what you have and lose so much more in the long AND short term!! "The Great Trek is a symbol of a nation's right to fight for its continued existence." So what about the ANC's right to do the same?
Lord, I don't know what to say: it seems that my parents just aren't listening. Still, I'll carry on loving them. Emotional healing has to take place, but I don't know how ..!

Stellenbosch
7 November 1988

Before I "run" to other people, I first want to talk to You. After my visit last night to Johann Kinghorn when he asked me again to write a contribution to a possible book: "Ons vir jou Suid-Afrika – Quo Vadis Afrikaners?" – (along with a bunch of famous/infamous people!?), my head was in turmoil.

Excitement about a possible opportunity, a privilege; uncertainty about my own ability, fear of the possible consequences in terms of the family and as a result of the "total onslaught" ideology; lack of knowledge about Africa, its history, etc. This was all an instant recipe for a sleepless night and a lack of productivity when it came to my MA thesis!

On the one hand it's really simple: a wonderful opportunity to sort out my convictions, to make a more tangible contribution. It's interesting that I just listened to Larry's tape this weekend, as well as to Martin Luther King Junior's sermons, which Larry gave me. That I had reread my report on the Africa tour and taken it to my parents.

For the first time in a long while I thought properly about the role You want me to play, about what reconciliation means. Again I felt so aggrieved about the way Afrikaners behave(d) towards their fellow-Africans, and I thought about the symbolic dimension of "Apartheid", but now my thoughts are starting to wander again ...

As I write I become more calm, Lord. Perhaps Johann's invitation is a test, another opportunity like at the house meeting in Wilgenhof in 1986, not to remain paralysed by embarrassment and uncertainty, but to get up and take a stand. Perhaps it's a test of my goal to become more involved in Africa, whether I'm *ready to risk all. (Perhaps that sounds a bit dramatic? Still, it's the first time I've ever faced a choice like this.)*

   Possible ideas for the article:

   Tragic ironies of the Afrikaner's history/situation:

- *SA as pariah of a world full of "expressive oppression".*
- *Afrikaners as the earliest "African Nationalists": struggle against colonialism, repression by English capitalism vs. Afrikaners' repression of the ANC.*
- *the DRC's emphasis today on the Church staying out of politics vs. Apartheid theology, involvement in the Poor White problem of the 30s and 40s.*
- *justification of "Separate Development", in terms of the dignity of people as members of various nations with rights to separate self-determination. They do not understand that the "self" in "self-determination" is defined by themselves, by a certain group on behalf of other people – in other words, that it's anything but self-determination. The "good intentions" at play make it a very dangerous arrangement – if there is "ingratitude", if not everyone wants to accept "self-determination", the "self-determiners" feel morally indignant and behave in a self-righteous way.*
- *being a Verwoerd: symbol of Apartheid, but precisely because so much pain and denial of human dignity is associated with "Verwoerd", it lends symbolic importance to my hesitant quest (Quo Vadis?) to find ways of restoring human dignity, my emphasis on our unity as Africans, instead of on differences between "Afrikaners" and "Blacks" – hence "Ons vir jou Suid-Afrika!..."*

The contribution to "Quo Vadis Afrikaners?" was never written after all. But I did carry on looking for an answer to this question. My overall awareness of the dangers of exclusive Afrikanership was acquired through conversations after the tour, particularly with Stian van der Merwe (a lecturer at the theological college in Lusaka where we stayed, at that stage on study leave in South Africa):

Stellenbosch
9 December 1988

It was very informative listening to Stian yesterday: the lack of freedom in South African society in spite of all the comforts, in contrast with Lusaka, "our roots

not lying in Europe". He emphasised that I must be patient in my struggle, that I mustn't fall into the same trap of "volk" in my attempts to give form to **Afrikanership** ...
But it wasn't until my return to Oxford that I really started to question the meaning of terms such as "Afrikaner" and "Africa", among others. My diary tells of the course in "sub-Saharan African politics" that I did in "Hilary Term" (February-March):

Rhodes House Library, Oxford
10 January 1989

It's wonderful to be sitting here in Rhodes House, surrounded by books on Africa, surrounded by wooden tables and wood-panelled walls – it's a completely different atmosphere. It's actually amazing that I'm sitting here so far from home and reading and learning about my own country and continent, writing a critical essay about African/Afrikaner Nationalism. It helps a lot to have some distance, as it gives me a better understanding of my country and its people, not forgetting that I'm actually also involved in the process of discovering myself...

12 January 1989

... Lord, sometimes it hurts me to read these things about the Afrikaner and his nationalism – "seek ye the political kingdom first" (Nkrumah) (?!) It's heartbreaking in retrospect to see what the consequences of my grandfather's policy were. On the one hand they were understandable, given the intellectual climate at the time, the Afrikaner's history in view of the British empire and English monetary power. One the other hand they were deaf to the cries of help of the ANC and others ...

Bless my studies of this complicated, sad history.

Summer Town House, Oxford
19 January 1989

Lord, it's late at night and I should have gone to bed a long time ago. But after last night's Bram Fischer memorial lecture by Beyers Naudé (Oom Bey), after my recent painful, revealing struggle with my own country's history, with the role of my grandfather, with myself, with what I want to/must do with all this knowledge, with You (I find it hard to believe that You have a plan for my life, for the world), after tonight's chat to Melanie (which made me realise all over again that I don't have to live in the shadow of my family, that feelings of moral guilt shouldn't get me down, that I don't have to be a Beyers Naudé or a Bram Fischer). Oh, Lord, after all these things, I just want to bow down before You and confess that it's all too big and too much for me ...

Attending a seminar on "African-American Social and Political Thought" at the Oxford Centre for African Studies' Summer school (also in 1989), exposed me further to the debates between "primordialists" and "constructivists" in the recent research about ethnicity and nationalism. The study of the complex history of social and political construction of, for example, Yoruba and Igbo identity in Nigeria, made me much more careful what I thought and said about "the Afrikaner", about the "primordial", ahistorical existence of "nations" that were created by God from the beginning, as it were.

The implications of these new insights, of a move away from "primordialism", were that I increasingly looked at South African society through new eyes. The definitions I learned at school, at home, in the media, were no longer so easy to accept. The official, clinical differences between a minority of "Whites" and a (large) majority of "Non-Whites", between "Coloureds", "Indians" and about 12 ethnic groups of "Black Africans", between a White "West" and a Black "Africa", could no longer serve as points of departure for understanding the past or the present, or for building the future.

Another implication was that I started placing many questions about my "Afrikanership" in brackets. "Who is the Afrikaner?", "What does it mean to be an Afrikaner today?", "Are Afrikaners losing their identity?", etc. My criticism of this kind of self-questioning was reinforced by Dr Shun Govender[10], shortly before I eventually joined the ANC. In a speech during a visit by a group of pigmentally challenged Stellenbosch students and lecturers to the WP Council of Churches in Cape Town, he more or less threw down the gauntlet:

10 Prominent Protestant theologian based in the Western Cape.

"You know, during all these years of the struggle against Apartheid we had little time to reflect, to write books and to do theology. We had to deal with one crisis after the other, we had to look after the poor, we had to try and protect and support those prosecuted for their fight against injustice ... Now it is your turn to act, to do the dirty work ... and our turn also to theorise..."

This just confirmed my conviction that from now on I should not define my "Afrikaner" identity in terms of one or other combination of unique characteristics (language, customs, view of history, etc.). That from now on I should see "Afrikanership" not as a noun but as a verb: an identification with "the people" and their problems, particularly in this southernmost corner of the continent of Africa; an identification with the "blood, sweat and tears" of the "struggle" for a non-racial, non-sexist, democratic South Africa.

But before this identification could take the form of a signature on the membership form of a liberation movement, I had to find out more about what the "A" in "ANC" stood for. It was important to move even further away from a philosophy based on race, which was how I tended to view the "African" in "African National Congress." Was the ANC just for pigment-rich Africans, or was there really a place in it for a pale-faced "Boereseun"?

In an attempt to find this out I held illuminating conversations with Blade Nzimande, Franklin Sonn, Carel Niehaus, Lourens du Plessis, Beyers Naudé, Breyten Breytenbach, Albie Sachs, Johann Kinghorn and others (including Nelson Mandela, with whom I had a brief but important talk, which I'll describe later).

In the first half of 1992 I also became involved again in one of the projects of the Centre for Contextual Hermeneutics[11], under Johann Kinghorn. The purpose of the Stellenbosch Economic Project was to make an interdisciplinary, intercultural contribution to economic policy formation, paying special attention to appropriate values that should be taken into account in the process. As a (political) philosopher with some exposure to economics and theology, and as part of my own effort to "complete" the 1988 tour report in particular, I tried to give shape to the theme "Culture, Gender and Development in South Africa" by means of consultations, workshops and more traditional research methods.

At this very time the Ghanaian/African-American philosopher Kwame Anthony Appiah's latest book was reviewed in the *Weekly Mail*'s Review of

---

11 Centre for contextual theology and value studies, located in the Department of Religious Studies, Unversity of Stellenbosch.

Books. After a phone call and a special trip to the distributors in Cape Town I finally got my hands on a copy of *In My Father's House: Africa in the philosophy of culture*. (Back in 1989, during the Oxford Centre for African Studies' Summer School, Appiah had read from a draft of this book.)

One of the chapters contained a fascinating discussion of the "Invention of Africa." Appiah tried to cast a critical light on the positive interpretation of "African traditions" by so-called "new Africans" – post World War II politicians, writers and (ethno-) philosophers (e.g. Kwame Nkrumah's concept of the "African Personality", Leopold Senghor's Negritude movement). Appiah tried to demonstrate how these "New Africans" were influenced by the "racial psychology" underlying the thinking of the 19th century "New World Africans", such as A Crummel and EW Blyden. This racial psychology manifested itself in "the belief that there are characteristically African ways of thinking" (Appiah 1992: 38). In this connection Appiah agreed with Paulin Hountjondi, a philosopher from Benin, who criticised "unanimism: the view that Africa is culturally homogeneous ... the belief that there is some central body of folk-philosophy which is shared by black Africans quite generally (38)." What is the basic problem with "unanimism", according to philosophers such as Wiredu, Hountjondi and Appiah?

"We will solve our problems if we see them as **human problems** *arising out of a special situation, and we shall not solve them if we see them as* **African problems**, *generated by our being somehow unlike others" (220) (emphasis added).*

I am inclined to agree with them, although my own experience teaches me that racism is a very slippery fellow indeed. To find that out you just have to talk to people who still believe there was (F W de Klerk), and is (Carel Boshoff), a big difference between race-based Apartheid and the policy of "Separate Development".

During the "Africa beyond liberation" conference in Potchefstroom at the end of April 1992, which I mentioned earlier, it was also fascinating to listen to the lively table debate between a Professor Sithole from Zimbabwe and a learned PAC supporter, about the existence or otherwise of an "African metaphysics". During his address on democratisation the professor reacted sharply to questions from the audience about why he failed to refer to the important contribution the "African political ethos" could make in this regard. "What do you mean by

'African political ethos?'" he asked. "If you say that it has to do with the ability to forgive even an Ian Smith, to achieve reconciliation within society as in traditional African communities, then I want to say to you: don't look in the past only for glory, look also for the misery. Furthermore, where was 'African metaphysics' during Idi Amin's rule, where was this 'African ethos' in the attacks on the Matabele recently?"

This answer and the questions it provoked led to a debate about the "African contribution" to democracy. The PAC supporter conceded that "democracy" could be viewed as "a universal system of governance with the consent of the governed". But that wasn't enough: "I believe that 'the participation of the governed' should be added to your definition. This should be acknowledged as an African contribution to the universal definition..." The professor was far from convinced, however: "Why do you place so much emphasis on 'Africanness'? I am sympathetic to the past, but I do not want to be preoccupied with the past...This 'African' contribution is not so different from what we have currently in many parts of the world..."

It wasn't (and still isn't) clear to me what side of the argument was the "correct" one. This type of experience did, however, lead me to place even more of a question mark over my understanding of the concept "African".

In retrospect, with my "fight for Jesus" in mind as well, I understand better why certain words leaped out of a page, as it were, just two weeks after this conference. I was rereading *In My Father's House*, and these words literally hit me between the eyes:

"But let me pursue Africa, finally, in Mudimbe's first novel, Entre les eaux ... *[In this novel] our protagonist is an African Jesuit, Pierre Landau...[who] is caught between his devotion to the Church and, as one would say in more Protestant language, to Christ; and the latter leads him to repudiate the official Roman Catholic hierarchy of his homeland and join with a group of Marxist guerrillas, intent on removing the corrupt post-independence state. When he first tells his immediate superior in the hierarchy, Father Howard, who is white, of his intentions, the latter responds immediately and remorselessly that this will be treason.*

'You are going to commit treason,' the father superior said to me when I informed him of my plans.

> *'Against whom?'*
> *'Against Christ.'*
> *'Father, isn't it rather the West I am betraying? Is it still treason? Don't I have the right to dissociate myself from this Christianity that has betrayed the Gospel?'*
> *'You are a priest, Pierre.'*
> *'Excuse me Father, I'm a black priest.' (Mudimbe, 1973: 18)*
>
> *It is important, I think, not to see the blackness here as a matter of race. It is rather **the sign of Africanity**. To be a black priest is to be a priest who is also an African; **and thus committed, willy-nilly, to an engagement with African suffering**" (Appiah 1992: 248) (my emphasis).*

Eventually, one Saturday in May 1992, with the autumn sunlight slanting through the window of a silent lounge – Melanie had taken our daughter to town – shortly after my second reading of Appiah's *In My Father's House*, I reached the point where I could sign a certain piece of paper.

Although it was very late in the struggle against Apartheid, although I placed a tick beside "Own Home" instead of "Shack behind a house" or "Squatter settlement" or "hostel", although my home language was Afrikaans, even though my job was to be an intellectual gadfly rather than a loyal member of any organisation, although the media (and possibly also the "terrorist communistic" organisation I was joining) might exploit the story, although my individuality would take a back seat (after all, I was a grandson of THE Architect of Apartheid), although some of his other children and grandchildren wouldn't be too happy, I believed and felt that becoming a member of the ANC instead of a passive observer, would be the right step on the road to afrika-nership: "To be an African ... (is to be) committed, willy-nilly, to an engagement with African suffering" (Appiah 1992: 248).

So what does it mean today to be an "Afrikaner"? As far as I'm concerned, in the first place it means: "to engage with African suffering", (i.e. to engage with suffering in Africa). In other words to identify with people, particularly "the people" in their suffering and oppression; to try to make a contribution to "Reconciliation, Reformation and Development" in an Africa that seems to be "beyond liberation".

Naturally to me being an "afrika-ner" also means fynbos and clean, cold mountain streams in the Boland mountains, wood fires and strong coffee in the bushveld, a deep blue sky, bright light and warm sunshine, singing, praying and discussing matters of the heart in Afrikaans ... But no longer apart from the suffering of my black fellow persons in particular. It meant I would no longer regard myself as separate from the sea of "separate anti-development" in which I lived. That I'd try not to see just the leafy, suburban side of Stellenbosch but the impoverished township of Kaya Mandi as well. For me, Afrikanership with a capital "A" was being replaced with a lower-case afrika-nership.

When I weighed up the existing political organisations in terms of their history, leadership, principles and policies, among other things, it was clear to me that such an afrika-nership could, in the political arena, best be expressed through the African National Congress. That was an important reason why I became a member of the ANC, though unfortunately I left it as late as May 1992 to join. Unfortunately as well, it wasn't a "Father Howard" but my own father (among others) who told me that as a result of this decision: "You are **a traitor** to the Afrikaner people."

Was I a traitor? It was a question that journalists asked after my decision became public and the international media pounced.

I don't know. Sometimes my "traitor's heart" (Malan 1990) says: "Yes, you are a traitor!" Sometimes I wonder: You say that "afrika-nership means that in the first place you identify with people and their problems in (southern) Africa ... but who benefits from this identification? Isn't this identification with others really for your own benefit in the final analysis? Isn't "engagement with African suffering" not perhaps a mask for sophisticated self-interest: "am I not, also, in the end, 'pleasing myself by doing good to others'?" (De Mello 1988). After all, sometimes it felt really great getting all the letters, phone calls, "Vivas" and handshakes, and all for an extremely belated decision? I told one journalist after the other: "I joined the ANC because I got tired of being a spectator, I wanted to get involved in the struggle for a democratic South Africa, and the ANC is the best alternative at present..." Was it really all about South Africa and democracy, or wasn't I just tired of feeling guilty, of no longer being part of a group? Or did I just want to do something to be remembered, to make my mark?

I have no easy answers to these questions. Sometimes a little voice inside me says: this story about African-ness is all very well, but in the final analysis isn't it just a story ... how far does your identification really go? Do you have a "**willy-nilly**" commitment?

"Willy-nilly" did help me, though, to stop questioning my choices all the time and to trust my "gut". But the choices I made didn't drive away all my fears. As an afrika-ner, choosing the ANC meant that sometimes I still felt like a (white) Afrikaner. Being a "comrade" and hearing all the "Vivas" helped a lot, but it didn't mean that sometimes I wasn't conscious of my lack of pigment − particularly when I drove past young people in Kaya Mandi who didn't know me, particularly after the death of Amy Biehl[12], particularly before the General Election. So it was still difficult for me to answer a journalist who asked: "Can you as a white person really identify with blacks in South Africa?"

Learning how to dream together and so build bridges across the apartheid between "African" and "Afrikaner" was liberating, but in the end "Africa" isn't just a concept, but a **continent**. A harsh, sickly continent with deep divisions, in which race plays an important part, particularly in South Africa − consciously and unconsciously, politically and economically. Becoming an afrika-ner is indeed a long, complex process.

This uncertainty about the depth of my "Africanness" was sometimes fanned by further questions about my involvement with the ANC, not just about the meaning of the"A", but also about the "N". What did the "National" in "African National Congress" mean? After a difficult process of liberation from Afrikaner Nationalism, what was I doing in another "nationalist liberation organisation"? This sort of question was expressed in a warning letter (8/7/92) from the leftist historian Baruch Hirson (we had met in Stellenbosch in 1991):

... then I read of your joining the ANC. It was a courageous move and showed that you had overcome some of your doubts. Yet I was afraid for you. Not physically − even though that must always be a factor in decision making of this order. I was afraid because I did not know if you had the ability to see that you had stepped out of one political laager into another. The nationalism you had once espoused had now been replaced by another nationalism (based on skin colour) but not affecting the very nature of the society that was to be erected.

How can one dispute the need for the majority to appear to take power and

---

12 An American exchange student and Anti-Apartheid activist who was brutally and tragically killed as a white person by a group of protesting youths in an African township outside Cape Town, on the day before she was to return to the United States.

replace the tyranny of the minority? Yet, if not seen in class terms, the vision is illusory. A new minority, without overt colour differentiation, will rule South Africa with all the old injustices intact ... And a black police force and army will do the suppressing as ruthlessly as the white police and army ... Am I being pessimistic?

... There is a further dimension that must be stated most emphatically. The ANC has shown itself to be ruthless in its dealing with its own members. We carried details of their activities in the camps in Angola, and then in east and central Africa in successive issues of Searchlight South Africa. *I do not believe, despite the commissions of inquiry, that the ANC has, or can, purge itself of the elements that commit this kind of atrocity. If they can it will be against the course of events of every nationalist movement in Asia, Africa or Latin America. Up till now the main perpetrators of wrongdoing in South Africa have been found among the whites. But what we have seen among the black vigilantes (from Crossroads onwards), or in Inkatha, or among the* comtsotsis, *or from within practically every black movement in the country does not lead me to believe that SA will prove exceptional.*

I think I had hoped that you might declare your sympathies with the majority in the fight for justice, but would have stayed aloof from a movement that cannot do other than become a suppressive force ...

After this, it was not easy to read the story of what happened after Pierre Landau had made his decision.

He was again accused of treason. This time, however, it was by the rebels, his comrades. They intercepted a letter in which Landau begged his bishop to support the rebels' cause in order to win them back to Christ. Landau was sentenced to death. While he waited for his execution he still struggled with the question: "What does it mean to be an African?" He was, however, saved from execution because the camp was attacked by government troops.

Intervention by the bishop and a brother's powerful connections with the modern state saved Landau from the fate of a captured rebel. Pierre Landau withdrew from the world and became a monk ... (Appiah 1992: 250).

Sometimes this former "Soldier for Jesus" feels he'd like to follow Landau's example. Sometimes when I consider the vast gulf between the pietistical, individualised heaven proclaimed in certain churches and the desolation of the Cape

Flats, then it seems to me that many Afrikaners are indeed imitating the last part of Landau's life. At least it looks as if many of "our people" in the "new South Africa" are continuing with our separate development on this earth. Perhaps the reduction of the size of the same old Apartheid names on the walls of buildings in Stellenbosch University is a symbol of a slightly amended continuation of Afrikanership, of a more restrained, less conspicuous but still "white" life in South Africa. Perhaps I'm not the only traitor?

That's why I cannot be content with "afrika-nership" as a symbol of solidarity, as a process of identification with "the people" and their problems in (southern) Africa. But it is the first step, particularly for a pigmentally challenged person with an Afrikaner Nationalist background. But it's not the end of the story. To me it seems eminently practical to emphasise the richness of pluralism in order to overcome the misery of apartheid. Not to deny the problematic political, sociological, economic weight of my lack of pigment, particularly in a post(political) Apartheid South Africa. But at the same time to learn to exploit the treasure trove of religious, linguistic, professional, ethnic, family, generational and regional variety in all its complexity. Then the difference between the smells in a sangoma's consulting room in Harare, Khayelitsha, and my doctor's rooms in Stellenbosch, the difference between the taste of strong coffee in the bushveld and home-brew beer in Kaya Mandi, the differing sounds emanating from a township club and an opera house, the difference between "white" and "coloured" Afrikaans, the difference between services in an Anglican or Dutch Reformed church and a Zionist church, etc. – all these differences will no longer be a threat, but enriching.

Even if it doesn't always feel as if I'm being enriched; even though I struggle to master the click sounds in the Xhosa language; even though I feel nauseous when I see the bakkie full of sheeps' heads in Kaya Mandi on Friday afternoon; even though it's shocking to drive through the Venda countryside to find the place where yet another "witch" has been cut up; or to see a tribal headman's wife kneel in the dust when she addresses him; an appreciation of the complex cultural variety of this corner of the African continent makes it much more difficult to use collective terms such as "Africa", "white", "black", "African/Afrikaner."

And then one day I got a phone call from an elderly Afrikaans woman. Despite her age I lost my temper with her. Perhaps it isn't so easy to escape the limitations of my afrika-nership, to get rid of my traitor label.

"Good evening, is that Mr Verwoerd speaking? ... Are you the one who's with the ANC and took part in a programme for British TV? ... I recently saw the programme in England."

I was half expecting her to congratulate me, or wish me luck for the future, but then she continued:

"I want to tell you I was very upset about the things you said ... You have disgraced our country! I saw you walking the streets of Kaya Mandi and telling the whole world how bad things were in the black townships, how bad we white people are ... Now I want to ask you: if you're so worried about the suffering of the blacks, why are you still living in Paradyskloof, why don't you go and live with the people in Kaya Mandi?"

Again I had no simple answers. So, aren't I still a traitor? Like a typical philosopher (or politician) my answer is: yes and no. Yes, because even though I sometimes have a lot to say on political platforms, I still have a lot to learn, through the ANC among other means, about what it means to be an African (albeit a pigment-poor, middle-class one) in Stellenbosch, in South Africa these days. No, because I'm trying to argue, again, that by holding on too tightly to the (white) capital "A", **"the Afrikaner IS losing his identity"**. No, because in my journey from Afrikanership to afrika-nership it feels as if I have lost much less than I've gained in terms of this source of my identity.

My clearest recollection in this regard was the recitation by Sandile Dikeni (a "people's poet") of a poem **in Afrikaans** by H Fagan, **dating from the 1930s**, during my first public ANC meeting in Parow City Hall. Although Fagan's emphasis on "volkere" (peoples) and "being white" now leaves me uncomfortable, that night I couldn't hold back the tears. I couldn't think of a better, more hopeful note to end this story on, for now:

NKOSI SIKELEL I-AFRIKA

Uit duisende monde word die lied gedra
Ek sluit my oë, soos 'n serafskoor/ val daardie stemme strelend op my oor:
Nkosi sikelel i-Afrika
Ons vra U seën, o Heer, vir Afrika/ Ek kyk, en sien die skare voor my staan;
Zoeloe en Kosa, Soeto en Sjangaan,/ en ek 'n Blanke – vele volkere, ja – /

105

almal verenigd om Gods seën te vra op net een tuiste, net een vaderland, /
want die Alwyse het ons saam geplant / en saam laat wortel in Suid-Afrika

Nkosi Sikelel i-Afrika – seën, Heer, die land wat vele volkere dra.

HA Fagan

NKOSI SIKELEL I-AFRIKA

The song is carried from thousands of mouths
I close my eyes; like a choir of seraphim/ those voices fall soothing on my ear:
Nkosi sikelel i-Afrika

We ask your blessing for Africa, oh Lord/ I look, and see the multitude standing before me:
Zulu and Xhosa, Sotho and Shangaan, /and I a white man – many nations, yes – /
all united in asking God's blessing on one home, one fatherland /
Because the All-wise has planted us together/ and let us take root in South Africa.

Nkosi Sikelel i-Afrika – Bless, oh Lord, the country of many nations.

HA Fagan

Chapter 4

From grandson to "prodigal son"

South Africa is a country of many baffling contrasts.
There have been few societies in history in which so much dedication for the promotion of a cause has been manifested by one section of a society while another section complained so persistently to be suffering from a sense of indignity and pain as the result of politics ostensibly designed for their long-term benefit.
Between the euphoric vision of Dr Verwoerd and the resigned apathy of a pass-law offender on his rapid progress through the magistrate's court stood a vast gulf of apparent incomprehension.

T.R.H. Davenport, A Modern History of South Africa.

Responsibility is not a concept belonging to the natural sciences, where no later event can alter an antecedent state of affairs,
but is concerned with meaning and significance, which ... may be reassessed and reinterpreted at a later date...
In so far as we take pride in what our predecessors have done, and enter into their achievements and make it a constitutive part of our identity,
we also identify with the bad things they have done,
and make their misdeeds our misdeeds
for which we must answer.

J.J. Lucas, Responsibility.

Growing up as a grandson of Dr HF Verwoerd, in the South Africa of the past three decades, meant that I felt the "baffling contrast" mentioned above more and more. Until I was 20 or so I largely shared Verwoerd's vision, via my family, my volk and the Voortrekkers. During this period I did, however, try to run away sometimes (literally and figuratively) from an ever-present noose around my own individuality. It was only late in my university career and overseas in particular that I started to become deeply aware of the pain behind the apparent apathy of pass law offenders, among others. In the process I started to understand something of what the word "Verwoerd" symbolised for most South Africans, and others. But "Verwoerd" was also my surname, THE "Grand Architect of Apartheid" was also my grandpa Hendrik!

For a long time I was paralysed by the confusing, vast gulf between Dr Verwoerd's vision and a pass offender's perspective. For a while I was laid low by a destructive, often oppressive sense of guilt. Then, eventually I (and Melanie) began consciously to actualise the positive potential of being a Verwoerd, particularly at this stage of our country's history. Instead of a crippling burden, I experienced my connection to the Verwoerd family in some ways as a liberating asset. From my identification with my forefathers I accepted the responsibility to try to make a contribution – to reconciliation instead of separation.

That is one of the reasons why I signed a membership form and started to make good on the promise – along with pass law offenders, within the ANC, at election meetings – to try and help eradicate the vision AND the pain of Verwoerdian Grand Apartheid.

Unfortunately this decision made Dr Verwoerd's eldest son terminate his third son's family membership (temporarily, at least). Unless I "came to my senses", apologise for my "idealistic straying", unless I showed remorse for the painful consequences my choice had on my family, from now on he would regard me as a "prodigal son".

I can't do justice to the story of how a chasm arose between my father's perspective and mine by only reflecting on my Christian pilgrimage and my little "afrika-ner Great Trek". I need to slow down and trace the path that took me from the bosom of my family to the astounding, liberating experience of hearing people shouting "Viva, Verwoerd!" at ANC election meetings in 1994.

It still feels ironic to be writing these words, almost 30 years after Dr Verwoerd was assassinated. I was about two-and-a-half when it happened. I didn't know him personally, but there is a fading, crumpled picture of him sitting with a little boy in a yellow suit on his lap, feeding me with a bottle while he smiled down at me (it was taken during a photo session for *Die Huisgenoot* magazine in September 1964). In spite of a lack of first-hand memories I grew up with a strong, positive image of his enduring presence. (Perhaps that's why a dramatisation – as I am writing – of his assassination by Tsafendas[1] on TV left me with an unexpected feeling of pain? Perhaps that's why I suddenly felt a bit isolated from comrade Thabo Mbeki when he said with so much conviction: "Yes, we were very happy when we heard about Verwoerd's death ... Tsafendas became a hero of the people ...")

You couldn't miss grandpa Hendrik in my parents' house. In the lounge/dining-room, near the entrance hall, in a place of honour, hung an almost life-size painting of Dr HF Verwoerd. Round the corner the family crest also hangs nowadays, with his famous words as a motto: "Create your own future." Every available book about Hendrik French Verwoerd can be found in my father's study. Although he isn't a man of many words, his (and the rest of the family's) deep admiration for Dr Verwoerd, as a parent and as a leader, was evident to me from an early age. At family gatherings we watched black and white films about his political career. The thousands of people who waited at the airport to welcome him and Ouma Betsie back when they withdrew the Republic of South Africa from the Commonwealth made an especially great impression on me. At these gatherings Ouma Betsie and the children would also talk about his dedication and firmness of principle as a statesman, his warmth towards the family, his concern about the welfare of the people who worked for him.

My initial impression of my grandfather was also formed by a book that stood on all his grandchildren's bookshelves, a book literally crammed with positive pictures. (As a child Melanie also became very familiar with this book on her grandparents' farm in the Transvaal, and years later it would make her look at me through different eyes.) When I page through this photobiographical tribute published by Voortrekker Press in memory of Dr Verwoerd, so many years and so many miles down the road, I find it a disturbing, if familiar experience:

Right at the start a smiling, white-haired man is giving a flower to a happy Ouma Betsie (this photo also hangs in my parents' bedroom); a photo of the building on the corner of Jacob van Lennepkade and Da Costa Street, Amsterdam,

---

1 An illegal immigrant, working as a parliamentary messenger, who was responsible for the assassination of Dr HF Verwoerd on 6 September 1966 in Parliament.

where he was born on 8 September 1901; then one of the earliest family photos in South Africa (Wynberg, Cape Town 1907); "Dr Verwoerd as a six-year-old lad," together with his father Wilhelm Johannes Verwoerd, his mother Anje (née Strik), his brother Len; a picnic for theological students at Gordon's Bay in 1921 and a walk along the beach, with Betsie Scoombee among others; a "Junior Day" at Stellenbosch, with a doll in his arms which he had to rock to sleep in front of a crowd of students; under that the 1923 Students' Council with HF Verwoerd in the middle (MA, Chairman); the postgraduate sociology class of 1936, with Professor HF Verwoerd; Dr Verwoerd speaking as editor-in-chief of *Die Transvaler* in 1937; the union congress of the Herenigde Nasionale Party in 1945, under the banner "Save South Africa from Communism"; police and rioters outside the hall: "Dr Verwoerd didn't escape unscathed, as he was hit by a brick on the shoulder"; election day 26 May 1948 with posters on the walls: "Alberton, vote VERWOERD, HNP" (he lost by 171 votes to Marais Steyn of the United Party); a family photo on the farm Wonderfontein – parents with six children and a dog – eldest son Wilhelm was the photographer); Dr Verwoerd and Dr WMM Eiselen visit "Bantu towns" in 1950, shortly after he became Minister of "Native Affairs"; Dr Verwoerd speaking in Leeudoringstad's new township, in front of a crowd of black faces in Windhoek township, discussions with "Bantu leaders" in 1953; my parents' wedding in 1954 – "I'll just baptise you with the confetti," Dr Verwoerd was apparently saying to the bride; "The Basothos have always had great respect for Dr Verwoerd. In 1957 he addressed a meeting of Basothos at Witzieshoek wearing a traditional Basotho hat"; on the steps of the Senate building (surrounded by middle-aged white men) – "2 September 1958: Dr Verwoerd elected leader of the National Party and Prime Minister of South Africa"; a smiling Dr Verwoerd "with a number of admirers during the Festival of the Covenant at Blood River in 1958"; an honorary doctorate was conferred on him on 29 July 1959 by Stellenbosch University; a bloody face after the first attempt on his life on 9 April 1960 ... "a large crowd of students gathered at the University of Pretoria for a scripture reading and to give thanks that the Premier had escaped death ... from all corners of the country a grateful people sent thousands of letters, telegrams and other tributes to Dr Verwoerd"; my father, mother and the other children who lived in Pretoria standing together on the stoep of Libertas – they had come to "enjoy Sunday dinner with their mother and father, as usual"; in front of a big crowd on Church Square after the results of the referendum were announced; in front of a SABC microphone: "South Africa stands on the brink of becoming a republic. We are not looking for enemies among the other countries, we are only looking for friends. For our population, white and black, we desire happiness and peace"; 20 March 1961, a crowd of about 50 000 people at Jan Smuts Airport: "South Africa has triumphed .. we have freed ourselves from the yoke of the Afro-Asian countries which make up the Commonwealth...We no longer feel at home in the Commonwealth"; lying on the ground in his suit: "Dr Verwoerd relaxes with Punch, the bulldog he received as a gift from an admirer in London"; the family at Betty's Bay; a proud fisherman with his giant tuna, finally bagged after a two-hour struggle in False Bay; "the enthusiastic angler at Robben Island" (?); one of the last family photos, 8 September 1964 (this time the little boy in the yellow suit is sitting on his mother's lap, without a bottle); with one of his Jersey cows, Patrys, at Stokkiesdraai, the farm on the banks of the Vaal River; Election Day 30 March 1966: "Dr Verwoerd addresses voters at 4.05 am ... In the election the National Party achieved the greatest victory in the political history of South Africa by winning 126 of the 170 seats in Parliament"; "We will not sacrifice this Republic and its independence and our way of life. If we are forced to by aggression, we will defend it with all that we have at our disposal" (Festival address, 31 May 1966); 18 July 1966, Liberia and Ethiopia's allegations against South Africa concerning South West Africa rejected by the world court: "... we see this as an incentive to rededicate ourselves to our guardianship of the less developed peoples of South and South West Africa"; 2 September 1966, a meeting with chief Leabua Jonathan of Lesotho, "the first meeting between a South African premier and the leader of a black state was widely welcomed and seen as the start of a new era in the relationship between white and non-white states in Southern Africa"; "A day of mourning – 6 September 1966", his body under a blanket outside the parliament building in Cape Town; Saturday 10 September, "more than 250 000 people gathered in Pretoria to pay their last respects to their Prime Minister and leader"; my mother, holding Hendrik junior by one hand and Dirk (my second eldest brother) by the other, Uncle Daniel and Aunt Rina, Auntie Anna and Ouma Betsie – in black and with sad, sombre faces beside the coffin, in front of the entrance to Heroes' Acre.

Besides the momentos in my parents' house and books (including of course my history books at school, which told more or less the same story as the commemorative album mentioned above), my impressions of Dr Verwoerd were also formed by his presence at the places where we went on holiday. His beach house at Betty's Bay (with a wooden house for his bodyguards nearby), as well as the house on the banks of the Vaal river, Stokkiesdraai, (where my grandmother continued to live until a few years ago), provided evidence that "the volk" and other admirers didn't only send him their handiwork that time he was recovering from the first attempt on his life. Paintings and decorations on the wall (as well as the tail of that whopping tuna), books on the shelves, items of furniture, springbok pelts on the floor, cutlery and glasses told the story of an exceptional grandfather. Even today at Betty's Bay the occasional caller stops by just to look at Dr Verwoerd's house.

With the "new South Africa" still in its infancy in September 1994, the trail of remembrance of HF Verwoerd is not limited to private family places. The HF Verwoerd Building opposite parliament is now 120 Plein Street, but at Stellenbosch University his name still appears on the Accountancy building (albeit in smaller letters than of yore). The HF Verwoerd airport in Port Elizabeth and the giant HF Verwoerd dam have now been renamed, but there is still the odd hospital and high school bearing his name. In a dusty office in rural Venda there's still a big photo of Verwoerd on the wall, and headman Davhana will show you the tree that Dr and Mrs Verwoerd planted when they visited there many years ago, after they'd all enjoyed a cup of tea together ....

There are many other people who remember Dr Verwoerd well and have stories to tell about him. I used to find that before I made my decision to join the ANC, people in the countryside, and Afrikaners in particular, would warm to me when I introduced myself, and invariably trot out an anecdote about "our greatest leader ..." I was often implored: "Don't ever be ashamed of your grandfather, do you hear?" Usually these conversations were concluded with an account of what exactly they were doing on that day in 1966 when the horrific news of his murder came over the radio, and how they (and often their servants, as well) mourned his death. The faded newspaper and magazine articles from that time (most in Afrikaans, but a few in English) do in fact tell a story of a time of great mourning for many people.

This story stands in "baffling contrast" to one that appeared on the front page of *Die Burger* precisely 28 years later (10 September 1994). A crane in the centre of Bloemfontein removing the giant statue of Dr Verwoerd ... and on the next page, a few (pigment-rich) people dancing on the heart of the "man of granite" (as he was known during his lifetime to his opponents/enemies).

The face of the statue looked familiar, and it vaguely reminded me of my grandfather. I did not know the faces of the people who were dancing, but in all probability we had signed the same membership forms. I did not know what to **feel** when I looked at the photo. On the one hand I wanted to join in the dancing, but on the other hand ... perhaps blood is indeed thicker than water? Was my "africanity", my afrika-nership being watered down by this family blood? Parts of me can really understand why some people, like my father, feel so upset. (It makes me wonder about the possibility of reconciliation – *Die Burger*'s journalists also wonder, of course.) I also know more or less, for the last few years anyway, why my "comrades" (quite possibly pass offenders until recently), can't let an opportunity slip by to trample THE symbol of Apartheid underfoot. As a comrade from the Cape Flats said:

I hope this doesn't upset you, but do you know what we did when we got the news of Verwoerd's death? We took off our shirts and danced with joy in the streets, along with our neighbours and friends.

By July 1993, when this conversation took place, I was no longer so shocked to hear Peter's story. After a painful process of re-education, specifically concerning Dr Verwoerd, the contrast between tears of grief and tears of joy, on the same day, were no longer so paralysing for me. My identification with Peter's story, with the pain behind his day of jubilation, did, however, emphasise the contrast between my father's perspective and my fist in the air at an ANC meeting. Peter's sensitivity and appreciation for the symbolism of this fist, however, confirmed for me the creative potential of my decision to join the ANC.

But let me return to the "painful process of re-education" and the "paralysis" that preceded this decision. (By doing this I hope to make some sense of the contradictory feelings I experienced when witnessing the victory dance of a couple of comrades as late in the day as September 1994.)

By the end of my high school years, as a critical awareness of my

Afrikanership began to develop, my positive pictures of Dr Verwoerd began to look a little murky. My reaction to this was to look away, to try to evade the expectations of "true Afrikaners", as well as the increasing criticism I heard from various quarters. I attempted to flee from the confusion and guilty feelings. This is one of the reasons why I broke a family tradition and went to Wilgenhof hostel instead of Dagbreek – the hostel where former Prime Ministers stayed. And it was one of the important factors behind my enthusiastic "Fight for Jesus" as a student at Stellenbosch.

One of the few diary entries I made for 1984 was written at the end of this escapist phase, although to a great extent it was just the beginning of the confusion I felt as a grandson and as a white Afrikaner between the images of a famous leader of his people (for some) and a notorious Apartheid leader (for most).

Betty's Bay
28 December 1984, 22h15

Finally, after turning everything over in my mind, I've decided to write down some of my thoughts again. The circumstances are very favourable for this: Dvorak's New World Symphony in the background, mixed with the restful, familiar hissing of gas lamps, with Ouma Betsie sitting beside me reading at the table. I'm feeling good because we've had such a meaningful conversation tonight. For a long time I've wanted to talk to her about all the political turbulence these days and how she sees the future. I particularly want to know more about her past with granddad and the origins of the policy of separate development – from a personal point of view.

I was really happy that she tried to understand my situation and also the complexities of the current situation in our country. I found it striking that she spoke out of fear that the blacks by sheer force of numbers would threaten the right to self-determination of the small group of whites. She firmly believes that the only solution is to give every people – white, black, coloured and Indian – an area where they can govern themselves. It's the only way to preserve a national identity and hand it on to succeeding generations. She also emphasises that things might have been very different today if Grandpa hadn't been taken away from us right at the start of the implementation of his policy.

114

She and I differed on many of the topics we spoke about, but what I really appreciate about her is the love she has for our people, our traditions, our self-reliance. (Like this morning when we cleared the path to the cafe, of all the litter, or when we pulled out the hakeas and other invasive, alien vegetation growing round the house.)

I can't really express what I'm trying to say in words. Perhaps it's just a feeling of self-respect, respect for your own people and your country, which radiates from her. A feeling of pride and belonging, which I encounter so little at Stellenbosch – on the contrary! Usually I'm overwhelmed with accusations against my whiteness, Afrikanerness, Christianity, surname. I admit that this pride can be carried too far, but among the young people in particular the lack of this pride is more often taken too far. Without it you get the feeling of spinelessness, drifting directionless and without an anchor.

Perhaps there isn't always a place for a feeling of security and safety within a philosophical nature. Still, it's nice for once in a while to say patriotic things, to write them, to feel them and perhaps even to believe them. Not to dismiss the whole lot the moment the Oranjewerkers [organisation working for a white homeland], the Conservative Party or the Afrikaner Volkswag are mentioned. (Which is what usually happens at Stellenbosch.) After all, you have to have self-respect. You have to ACCEPT yourself! You must have a frame of reference that allows you to have respect and understanding for other people and races.

This has all become really clear to me after all the writing and talking. Next year I really must take the trouble to study Grandfather's life and speeches in detail, to brush up on my knowledge of politics after the quite intentional drought in this area over the past few years. So I can get away from an exaggerated feeling of guilt and sensitivity to my family and people's past, present and future! I am just sick and tired of uncertainty and evasion when it comes to these things. I am tired of fearing being placed in a particular category, tired of not having an independent, well thought out point of view. (Easier said than done, I know!)

My new year's resolutions for 1985 would only really take shape in 1989/90, in the form of a mini-thesis at Oxford. This formal study was, however, preceded by a much more effective education process. On the student tour at the end of 1985, during the three months in the Netherlands in 1986, during the OCAS Summer

School in 1989, etc., people's experiences helped me to "study Grandfather's life in detail", but to "appreciate" it in quite a different way from the picture I was fed along with my mother's milk. Again, often whether I liked it or not, I listened to various people's stories about Dr Verwoerd. This time, however, I was confronted with so many people's negative associations with the name Verwoerd – from "Bantu Education", pass laws, Sharpeville, the banning of the ANC, to becoming a Republic, outside the Commonwealth.

In the "political letter" to my parents from the Netherlands, to which I've referred before, I mentioned a few of these opportunities at re-education.

... One of the many black people from South Africa and Namibia whom I've met at Caux was a Professor Marivati from Unisa (African languages). He is now involved in Black education. As a highly educated fellow-Christian (who had to endure a lot of stress as a result of his "commitment" to reconciliation and his willingness to work with Whites), he told me how the black people experienced Grandpa's education policy.

He told me some of the positive points that Father has mentioned, e.g. that Grandad tried for the first time to introduce general education for black children and not just leave it to the mission schools. He also told me, however, how terribly frustrating it was (is!) for them because they didn't really have any say in the policy. How initially they had compulsory instruction in Tswana or Zulu (Bantu education). Later, after a great deal of protest by black people because they were in effect being shut out of the Western (English) world and prevented from competing with whites on an equal basis, how subjects were taught half in Afrikaans and half in English. And when subjects such as Singing, Physical education, etc., were offered in Afrikaans in order to make up the quota, they were forced to teach History and Maths, for example, in Afrikaans and Biology in English. In the end, that was the spark that ignited the powder keg in Soweto in 1976.

Other coloureds and blacks have also told me how they experienced the "brick wall" of Dr Verwoerd (his firmness of principle, from our point of view): no openness to possible alternative ways of educating the community...I am not making an issue of whether their experiences were right or wrong, just that they (and so many others) experienced it like this....

Actually I am trying to say: Once again, as with Amor and Rudolf, I realised with a shock that the same South African reality, that Grandfather as a person, was and is experienced completely differently from what I've experienced thus far.

This type of exposure to other people's view of the architect of Apartheid naturally caused a great deal of conflict within the family and within myself. These conflicts became more intense after my "rebirth" in Holland.

My diary for 1988 helps to tell this part of the story:

Stellenbosch
7 November 1988

... I've recently started to realise (particularly as a result of the weak excuse I gave to get out of going to the Great Trek 150 Festival with my parents) that keeping quiet and compromising doesn't necessarily bring reconciliation. In fact, it builds emotional walls. In other words, on one hand I'm trying to place less emphasis on politics with my parents, but on the other hand it's not really working out as far as our relationships are concerned – politics cannot be divorced from other things. Love "in spite of", an ideal of reconciliation, easily becomes an excuse not to stand up and live out my religious convictions in honesty and humility.

What it comes down to in the end is that I am coming to You to seek wisdom and LIGHT – it's a matter that I want to raise with You in the first place: You led me to Oxford, to study PPE, to travel to other African countries; You placed me within a specific family for a specific purpose; I have dedicated my life to You ... (I don't always know what it means to say "You led me", or precisely what I understand by "You") – all these thoughts swirl through my head ...

Possible ideas for article about the tragic ironies of the Afrikaner's history:

... – Being a Verwoerd: symbol of Apartheid, but precisely because there is so much pain and denial of human dignity associated with the name "Verwoerd" it lends symbolic meaning to my hesitant (Quo Vadis?) search for ways to restore human dignity, my emphasis on our unity as Africans instead of differences between "Afrikaners" and "Blacks" – hence "Ons vir jou Suid-Afrika!"

Stellenbosch
18 November 1988

... Yesterday was another low point, after the previous week's rapid progress with my MA – terribly warm, slept badly before Melanie's exam, went riding with her in Jonkershoek and had a wonderful talk about politics: about our regret over the CP's idealism, over the lunatic Wit Wolf[2] who shot a number of black people in cold blood the day before yesterday.

I don't know what to say. Lord, I get so angry about the racism that some people try to disguise by saying: "We are not racist, we're just race-conscious," angry with my family with their conservative, moral, Christian pretensions. The theory of "Grand Apartheid"/"Separate Development" is/was only accessible to a small group of people, so it will never succeed ...

Stellenbosch
21 November 1988

What a lovely weekend. It was fantastic to be in the unspoilt surroundings of Betty's Bay – to sit and read with the sound of the sea in the background and the gulls cawing. It was a tonic for my soul: running along the beach, swimming in the lagoon, lightheartedness mixed with serious philosophising and sharing the frustrations I'm experiencing with my family.

Love, love, but also honesty. My frustrations and paralysis at my parents' home are not the result of politics: they are caused by my lack of honesty, by the fact that I keep quiet too much ...

In the midst of all these conflicts my New Year's resolutions at the end of 1984 raised their heads again:

Stellenbosch
28 July 1988

... It was a strange experience, after Melanie and I had just been discussing it last week, to be told by Pa Phillip that he thinks I should write a book about my grand-

---

2 A small group on the extreme white right wing, whose most notorious member is Barend Strijdom, convicted for the cold-blooded murder of a large number of black South Africans, later released as part of an amnesty agreement between the NP and the ANC.

father one day. In a sense I owe it to myself – it's a tremendous challenge. Perhaps it's an example of opportunities and responsibilities that are given to me because of my family ties, my education, religious and political convictions, my attachment to Africa! The possibilities excite and frighten me, oh Lord ...

Stellenbosch
5 December 1988

... Yesterday was a difficult Sunday: strange emotions after reading the booklet about great-grandfather Wilhelm Johannes Verwoerd. Father says the book isn't really to be taken seriously. Still, I was struck by the picture of a simple, dedicated, loving man (my mother says his wife, Ouma Anje Strik, was a very strange bird indeed). According to one dominee my great-grandfather was not someone who discriminated against people on the grounds of race, language or group!? It's an example worth following, but in different circumstances – i.e. the "Boerevolk" aren't my top priority.

Yesterday afternoon I also looked at some of the other books in Dad's study: these books are written from either an over-critical English perspective, or from an Afrikaner perspective: "the man who never made any mistakes". There is a 600-page doctorate on just the Johannesburg periods in Dr Verwoerd's career, without a single interview with a black person, or a single critical reference in the bibliography! This makes me very excited about a gap that can be exploited – I pray for Your wisdom and love!

Betty's Bay
17 December 1988

It's wonderful to be here in Betty's Bay all by myself on a Saturday night (like I was a few years ago), with the wind blowing a gale.

Lord, after the many conversations I've had and all the thinking I've done recently about Africa and being an "African/Afrikaner", and about the book(?) on my grandfather, on Apartheid ideology, it feels strange sitting here in his house, with Transvaal holidaymakers admiringly taking photos. Especially after reading in Davenport's Modern History of South Africa, *after the Great Trek celebrations*

119

on the Day of the Vow yesterday, it hurts me so much to read this history and realise what a one-sided Christian National education I had. I got a distinction for history in Matric – for studying half of my country's history!

Shortly after this, during my "second life" at Oxford (from January 1989 to the middle of 1990, accompanied by Melanie), the most important phase of my re-education began, specifically with reference to Dr Verwoerd. Once again I needed a midwife or two. Once again this stubborn horse had to be brought to water, before I could look another facet of my self in the eye!

In my first term back in a cold, dark England "Sub-Saharan African politics" was on the menu. An unexpected set of coincidences meant that at the same time I really came to grips with the subject of my grandfather. In this process, in the midst of intense feelings of guilt and even shame, it wasn't always easy to keep a cool head. A few extracts from my diary in this period testify to this:

Oxford
23 January 1989, 00h30

After a time of seeking it feels as if we have reached calmer waters.
  Important thoughts:
- *part of my uncertainty is caused by legitimate, complex, important choices.*
- *I am also studying SA politics/history which I first became really familiar with after my conversion in Holland. It feels as if I know nothing, so I feel unsure of myself. Even more important: I feel involved with this history, it makes a strong moral appeal to me. It produces a feeling that I must react, I must do something about it. At the same time I'm frightened and confused in terms of my judgment/ criticism of what happened, as well as my future direction ...*

Oxford
24 January 1989

... This afternoon after my tutorial I started thinking again, in spite of the little time left before the next economics tut. Sigh. In any case, important new insights:
- *studying SA politics inevitably gives me a great deal of food for thought,*

particularly with my muddled philosophy and family background.
* *considering the complexity of the matter, the complex relation between theory and practice, my fear of getting actively involved in "the liberation struggle", my caution – which makes me carry on swotting so I don't have to openly refuse to do my national service – considering all these things it surely isn't surprising that I've landed up in a moral labyrinth or a mental whirlpool, from which it feels as if I can't escape. That's why I so often feel drained of energy, why I don't want to get involved in the present...*

Oxford
7 February 1989

Another spring day, despite the fact that it's only February, with daffodils and blossoms already coming out. During a Sunday walk in the University Parks it was pretty to see patches of flowers blooming apparently from nothing. And out of the blue the letter from John Stewart [then editor of Optima *magazine] arrived. He heard from Johann Kinghorn about the tour report I wrote last year, and now he wants me to contrast my experiences in Africa and my present political viewpoint with those of my grandfather! This commission (and the financial carrot – R3 000 for two people trying to live on one Rhodes Scholarship!) made me feel excited and scared all at the same time.*

Perhaps it's the incentive I need to really start reading about that period, about his personality (in spite of the limited perspective here in England), to use all the hours of brooding and struggling with the subject to make a cautious contribution to breaking down Afrikaner stereotypes, to start building bridges. It's the first time I've had such a chance, Lord. It can be used fruitfully, or misused. Actually, back in South Africa I'd already made the decision to be honest about my views/quest, also with respect to my family.

Thank you, Lord, for the privilege of being here so I can get the necessary distance, to learn about my country from another perspective. Thank you, Lord, that I don't have to be ashamed of who and what I am – Afrikaans, Verwoerd, White, Your child, in spite of my incomplete insight, etc. With the necessary realism about fellow South Africans I shouldn't have to avoid them, like yesterday at the seminar on "people's courts".

Afrikaner-bashing is also not a solution. If I don't participate wholeheartedly in the struggle, if I'm not ready to spend six years in jail etc., this doesn't mean that I/we aren't looking honestly for a solution. And if that makes me naive, it doesn't mean I can't make a contribution ...

My decision to accept John Stewart's invitation was made easier by new research that had just been completed at Oxford, specifically about the period within which my grandfather's political career fell. My tutor for Sub-Saharan African politics, Gavin Williams (a former South African, and a former student of Professor Degenaar), was involved in the work of Debbie Posel, John Lazar and Adam Ashforth (see bibliography). In our tutorials (in Afrikaans and English) our conversation naturally turned to Dr Verwoerd. Williams encouraged me to look at the abovementioned theses because they painted a more complex picture of the development of Apartheid, the conflicts **within** the NP "alliance" (Lazar) and thus also Verwoerd's role.

Considering my full academic programme at Oxford I had to make time to do this reading. Fortunately, in the PPE course there was the option of writing a mini-thesis on a subject of your own choice. John Stewart's letter made me look at this option with new eyes. I would have had to do research for his article in any case, so this way I could kill two birds with one stone:

Oxford
8 February 1989

...Thank you for the opportunity at last (after 25 years!) to put my thoughts about HFV, Apartheid and being an Afrikaner into writing. I feel like a sponge that has absorbed as much water as it can.

Thank you for enabling me to write in a searching way, without evading my commitment any longer, or knowing precisely what the implications will be for the future! This decision and my tremulous resolutions give me new self-respect. I pray for wisdom and the necessary powers of discretion.

Little Rodd
Wales
13/05/89

... *It was quite a revelation to me when I started reading about HFV's youth last night (in between the irritating interjections from a terribly subjective biographer), and to see how he also experienced painful disillusionment, but in a completely different context; how his exposure to the terrible living conditions of poor whites in the suburbs of Cape Town while he was at University shook him and encouraged him to practise "practical patriotism" (Scholtz, 1974: 16-24) – What ironic parallels!*

Lord, please bless this project and grant me wisdom to carry it out, and I pray also for Melanie who is trying to maintain the balance!

Lord, it's disturbing to read how firmly principled he was – Christian National principles, which were based "on the truth". Is this why at the beginning of Scholtz's biography Ouma Betsie quoted the prophet Isaiah: "Look to the rock from which you were hewn" (Isaiah 51:1)? And the coloured man at Caux who told of his painful confrontations with the "man of granite"? (Or Gavin Williams who says his picture of HFV was always the cartoon with the telephone line in Dr Verwoerd's office that ran up the wall and disappeared into the roof?)

It is so difficult to criticise "firmness of principle" because then you can easily find yourself accused of being without principle yourself. But his firmness of principle, vocation and self-assurance were not like love as I understand it – You who are also Lord of the Sabbath, Paul who becomes like a Jew to the Jews, and for the Greeks like a Greek, etc. Firmness of principle versus legalism or inflexibility; when does integrity, honesty, pride, become a form of stubbornness? What about Your will, which is only revealed to us in pieces, like a puzzle in a mirror? People (of all colours!) who are more important than principles/ideologies?

Oxford
03/07/89

...*Thank you for the tremendous wisdom that flows from Laurens van der Post's Jung and the Story of our Time ... Thank you for their resistance to narrow vision, their emphasis on the positive potential of the unconscious, of the painful challenge of becoming an individual within the space of the "collective unconscious".*

I still don't understand everything, but it feels as if a window has opened up in my spirit which is letting a cool breeze blow over my furrowed brow...

Last night I thought about the dream of my grandfather: how frightened I was for him and how liberating it felt to start talking to him, to feel that people had misunderstood him, that he also didn't understand me!

Please bless the next few days, when I'll finally get down to writing the article ...

This article for John Stewart was completed a few months later after a few stops and starts, and I gave it to a friend to take back to South Africa. It was never published, though. I was apparently too academic and too qualified in my criticism, apparently too many of my dreams (and too little of my shame) were revealed there. There is, after all, a big difference when "the truth" is told by a Posel, Lazar or Ashforth and when Dr Verwoerd's white, middle-class grandson comes along in 1989 to complicate the picture an English-speaking South African readership has of the architect of Apartheid ...

The reality of this difference (and the symbolism of "Verwoerd") was succinctly brought home to me during the Oxford Centre for African Studies' Summer School in 1989. Right at the start, just after the first lecture about the philosophy of W E du Bois[3] (my first exposure to a black professor in a classroom, not to mention "African-American social/political thought"), while I was sitting peacefully dipping a biscuit in my tea a large, bearded African-American professor came up to me. He bluntly asked: "Tell me, are you related to Hendrik Verwoerd ... mmm, interesting ... was your grandfather a Nazi?"

My reply that recent research indicated to me that he wasn't QUITE as wicked as that wasn't received with much enthusiasm. The next day some of the visiting students and lecturers from America made it very clear to me that I was no longer welcome. The head of the Centre politely asked me to leave Jesus College for the time being. He was facing a boycott because of the presence of a white, Afrikaans Verwoerd. My bona fides would have to be checked, like those of other (more pigment-rich) people from South Africa.

A phone call or two, specifically with Dr Frene Ginwala[4], and the mediation

---
3 Leading African American writer, philosopher, activist at the turn of the twentieth century.
4 Prominent activist of the ANC in exile, currently Speaker of the National Assembly.

from people such as Dr Blade Nzimande (one of the course leaders), defused the situation. The contrast between the reaction of the Americans and the South Africans, who were prepared to defend the principle of non-racism even in my case, made a great impression on me. The professor's actions upset and inhibited me so much, however, that afterwards I was too scared to open my mouth (and I never did finish that biscuit).

I did try to express my emotions and thoughts in words, after the closing party back home. On one hand I was furious with myself because I hadn't got up, like some of the other people at the party, and told everyone just how much the South Africans' acceptance meant to me. On the other hand I was also encouraged by a conversation with a (pigment-rich) brother in the garden of Jesus College. He admitted that he was full of mistrust and even repugnance when he heard who I was. Fortunately he continued: "Now I see that you are not like your grandfather ... I feel different ... you have helped me to break down the wall between us." This type of experience made me realise that it might not be too late and gave me the idea of sending the following lines to the other South Africans on the course [even though I never got round to it, and when I read it now it sounds rather clichéd, it is an important part of the story]:

Oxford
11/08/89, 01h00

To my fellow South Africans: OCAS Summer School, Jesus College Oxford

There are so many things that I wanted to say to you tonight
There are so many conflicting emotions
blowing me around like a ship without a rudder
Why didn't I also stand up and share my pain, fear, hopes with you?
Why am I so afraid to stand up and sing and dance with you?
Perhaps because of so much Azanian blood and bitterness in the poems and songs (mainly by Americans)?
Perhaps because I don't/cannot really understand your tears – feel responsible for them – and therefore cannot laugh with you?
My Afrikaner nationalist history amidst the seductive beauty of Stellenbosch feels

indeed like a world apart from your cries for freedom.
Still, I want to thank you for accepting me as you did,
despite all your associations with Verwoerdian Apartheid.
I cannot ask you to forgive –
the struggle is not over, your suffering is too great...
I cannot take responsibility for all my people had done,
are doing
But in humility – as a fellow "Afrika-ner".
I can only ask you to accept my sincere apology...
I can assure you of my commitment to a new South Africa
Of my constant prayer that God will indeed
bless (South) Africa!

The article for *Optima* did in the end form the basis for the mini-thesis which was finally handed in in April 1990. By that time Melanie (among others) was sick to death of my struggle with Grandpa Hendrik's ghost. But in retrospect the struggle was well worth it.

In the mini-thesis I basically made use of a few theoretical distinctions in order to explain an (apparent) conflict of interpretations with regard to Dr Verwoerd's historical contribution – hopefully without excusing him.

This struggle made me understand why my grandfather was, and probably would always be, THE symbol of Apartheid to most South Africans and foreigners alike.

In *Let My People Go* (one of the books that had a great influence on me) Chief Albert Luthuli expresses this deep-rooted and justified perception as follows:

Of the men who have ruled South Africa ... no one has been the guiding mind behind so much negative and oppressive legislation. If any one man is remembered as the author of our calamity, it will be he (1982: 176).

In the thesis I tried to formulate it as follows:

A man of benign appearance, he both mesmerised and dominated his political followers to an extent not achieved by any of his Nationalist predecessors.

Intellectually, he stood head and shoulders above most of his contemporaries in Parliament, while his self-assurance and didactic manner led many to believe that he could conjure into being the political objectives of his fertile imagination. (Davenport, 1986: 389).

Given Verwoerd's political style and personality, the highly successful consolidation of power and support by Afrikaner nationalists between 1948 and 1966; the intransigent nature and relentless enactment of prominent features of Apartheid – such as the policies of residential segregation, the prohibition of interracial sex and marriage, the creation of a system of "Bantu Education" – and the high and increasing visibility of ideology in government policy and rhetoric, it is indeed tempting to take, what Posel terms, a "grand plan" approach to the development of Apartheid, with Verwoerd being the architect of this plan.

This picture strengthened my awareness of the positive, symbolic potential of the blood in my veins. At the same time the deepening of my historical consciousness gave me a better understanding of the political, social and economic limitations in which he functioned as a politician. This made my (moral) conclusions more humble and more tolerant. It also made me understand why outsiders' criticism of his actions was so ineffective. Why it was/is such a great temptation for my father, for example, to distinguish between "Apartheid" and "Separate Development" and to see the latter as a good policy that didn't work....

This process made it easier for me to live with a cautious distinction between criticisms of Verwoerd's politics – fundamental, moral and practical criticism of the policy which he so effectively defended – and an acceptance that my grandfather wasn't (as far as I could make out) a "Nazi".

Perhaps Alan Paton's conclusion to the question whether Verwoerd was blind to the consequences of his policies, or whether he blinded himself to them, is helpful in this regard:

"... in how far was he benevolent, or was he capable of malevolence? When I answer all these questions I cannot conclude that he was an evil man...That he was arrogant in his self certitude, I have no doubt. But I conclude that he deceived himself. He believed that he had solutions for the problems of Africa when he had not. What is more, in his search for these solutions, he had one overruling principle,

and that was the safety and the security of the Afrikaner volk." (Paton, 1989: 266-7)

What is clear, without Paton's help and without the benefit of hindsight, is that he deceived many others. Even today many supporters of the National Party are only pragmatically accepting that alternatives to Apartheid are not per definition a recipe for things and principles to fall apart. Recent developments are significant, but many still hold on to group rights, the principle underlying Separate Development. Together with, for example, the redistribution of land and wealth, this principle must change, I believe. Otherwise Verwoerd's ghost will continue to haunt South Africa on her difficult road to shared freedom.

This qualified (moral and political) judgment of Dr Verwoerd made me doubt, particularly at that time, whether it was possible for me to make sense of it all without appearing to justify his sins, albeit unconsciously. I think I succeeded, though, in converting destructive guilt feelings into a more constructive acceptance of responsibility. This process would take a long time. It was a gradual but decisive process that was further complicated by the often startling contrasts between my reflections on the past and my experiences in the present.

For example, while the Summer School was in progress my father paid me a short visit on the way to a conference in America:

Oxford
01/08/89

I am thankful to you that the Summer School episode turned out well, even though it was more tense than I would have liked to admit, with all the phone calls and the feeling of personal injustice. Perhaps I just don't like conflict and rather unrealistically want everyone to accept me ...

Thank you also for a blessed day on Saturday with my father. It felt funny meeting him here in England, to go for a pub lunch together and walk round Kew Gardens. It was great to talk to him, particularly to hear more about his life before and during the academy. But it was upsetting to hear his ideas on the past and future – Luthuli a communist????

What a contrast between the Summer School and his world! But I was born somewhere in between these two worlds and I want to live out my life (with Melanie) in your service there ...

And in February 1990 I was, on the one hand, experiencing history from my grandfather's perspective (and doing it in Rhodes House library, of all places, with the names of people who had died in the various wars – including the Anglo-Boer War – listed near the entrance, and a statue of Lord Milner – the man notorious – particularly among Afrikaners – for his "scorched earth" policy and the bringer of death to thousands of women and children in concentration camps!). On the other hand we were sitting expectantly in front of the television set, drinking champagne with friends and clapping when Nelson Mandela walked through the gates of Victor Verster prison, fist in the air! One day we looked at painful documentary material from the past ... things could have turned out SO differently! The next day I sat at a desk piled with books trying to make sense of Dr Verwoerd's life...

Oxford
12/02/1990

What joy! What exhilaration!
What an exciting day it was yesterday, and I felt so close to South Africa and its people (and problems). Nelson Mandela was freed!! The whole world rejoiced – except of course for the AWB and co., and the white people who looked on apprehensively as thousands of people sang and danced, certain that THIS was at last the beginning of the end of Apartheid.
Thank you, Lord, for this great moment. Perhaps for now it's enough to just be happy, for Mandela and his people. But it's not so easy. This is just the beginning of the long and difficult negotiation process that lies ahead. Perhaps it's hard for me to stare reality in the face, to realise that the future is no longer in the hands of the whites (perhaps it never was?), and that not only these whites are "my" people.
Lord, it feels petty to talk like this, but it is part of the way I'm feeling, particularly after being reminded constantly of the history of the last 27 years yesterday. Reminded of a grandfather who ignored Mandela's letter, who as prime minister played such a great part in these tragic events. I have already confessed

to my collective guilt in the past, but yesterday made it so much harder to write about HFV, and to try to contextualise him.

And I also feel sad that I never took the trouble to try and visit Mandela in jail. Perhaps my motives are not purely unselfish, but maybe it's not yet too late.

Last night, while we were still marvelling over the day's events, I clearly felt the baby kicking in Melanie's stomach!

Oxford
17/03/90

... This morning I had another clear dream in which I asked Nelson Mandela's forgiveness for my grandfather's share in his suffering, and that of so many other South Africans. I want to write and tell him about it. He's presently visiting Sweden. I pray for him, and I pray for our country and all its people ...

Shortly after this dream I actually got round to writing a short letter, believing "better late than never".

Dear Mr Mandela   *18 March 1990*

This is a personal letter that I have not only wanted to write for a long time, but feel compelled to write. For ages I have wanted to express my thankfulness to you for your inspiring example as a true statesman, and I want to underline my support for your dearly bought ideal of a nonracial democracy in South Africa. In a sense, that is the easy part of this letter.

Since your release the difficult part has become even more difficult. The more I see and read of you, the more I study our country's tragic history, the deeper my realisation of how different everything could have been, of my own people's guilt. And the more painfully I feel the responsibility and guilt of "the one man who would be remembered as the author of our calamity" (Chief Luthuli), namely Dr HF Verwoerd.

Naturally history – a long, unjust 27 year long incarceration and the part my grandfather played in that – can't be changed with a few words. But as an Afrikaner who benefited from Apartheid at the expense of other South Africans, as the grandson of the architect of "separate development" – the man who above all others was responsible for your suffering and the suffering of so many other people – I want to say to you: I am very, very sorry about what happened.

I can't ask for forgiveness on his behalf. In any case, such a request would easily sound meaningless because I understand so little of what you endured during the past few decades. What I can do is to assure you that my wife and I want to spend our lives trying to convert words of apology into deeds. To make South Africa a country of shared, humane freedoms, in place of Verwoerdian "separate freedoms" (for some). I sincerely hope that I will have the opportunity to talk to you personally about this. In the meantime I pray for God's blessings on you, your family and Africa.

The letter was an important step in a certain direction. But I was still doubtful about my own motives. The letter helped, but I still found myself often feeling guilty, and I often woke up in the morning feeling so numb that I could hardly get up. I was often too frightened to read the papers and see what was going on in South Africa, and I often tried to avoid my fellow South Africans ...

Once again I found spiritual solace in the pages of a book. This time it was Charles Elliot's *Praying the Kingdom: Towards a Political Spirituality*. My doubts over my motives were confirmed by Elliot's "bad news" about the various defence mechanisms people tend to use to handle their guilt feelings:

*To summarise the story so far: I have argued that when we face the facts of the world we are assailed by two psycho-spiritual reactions, **guilt** and **powerlessness**. These are extremely destructive in the way they interact ... [they are like] one of those spring-loaded, sharp-toothed traps concealed under leaves or thickets ... for there is a dynamism, a cruelty and a degree of concealment in the way guilt and powerlessness interact in our lives, which combine to make them a trap of the most dangerous variety.*

Dynamism first: guilt triggers a need to work out one's salvation...most of us, once seized by a sense of guilt ... seek to "put it right" ... We want to do something – something fast, dramatic and effective ...

We want to break out of our involvement in exploitation ... but we find that whatever we do to achieve that is vanity...So it seems as I demonstrate, or write letters to my political representative or newspaper ... And that burns me up. I'm left with my guilt unexpiated. And with my powerlessness and frustration unresolved ... I [usually, then] pretend that what I have done is making a difference ... or the unresolved tension goes into my unconscious, and there it plays merry hell ... That is the bad news (1985: 14, 8-10).

It came as something of a relief when I recognised the hidden, violent working of Elliot's sharp-toothed trap in myself. But I was encouraged by his "good news":

The good news is that both guilt and powerlessness can, paradoxically, form a rich humus out of which prayer for the Kingdom can grow abundantly. To change the image, a central skill in most martial arts is to use the destructive power of one's opponent to one's own advantage...

[This requires] **a full awareness of the object of guilt** *... As long as guilt is vague, half-acknowledged, shadowy, it will always constitute more of a threat than when it is fully explicated ...* **That is easier said than done** *...*

[But] is this not guilt writ large? Is it not the lower jaw of the trap with teeth freshly sharpened?

The gift of the Christian faith is precisely that it enables us to transcend that guilt. That does not mean that we pretend it isn't there or isn't loathsome in the sight of God and the sight of those who suffer as a result of it. It is all of that: yet we believe that, once we acknowledge what we can perceive of the full extent of our guilt ... we are offered a quality of life no longer dominated by the failings for which we have asked forgiveness. This is, however, **not a quick fix that makes saints of us at a stroke**. *Rather it is the promise of a new dynamic in our lives that allows us to confront the forces that makes us and our world so different from what God wills for them ... (1985:14-18) (my emphasis).*

Although in a sense this was old news for a former 'Soldier for Jesus', it was still good to hear it again particularly at that stage. This news was (and is) not an instant solution, though. It took a long time before the promise mentioned above became visible in our lives. It's still a struggle to recognise the trap, to confront one's feelings of guilt and powerlessness and turn them to good use.

A few months after I'd sent the letter to Nelson Mandela and read Elliot's liberating words (and the 2 February 1990 speech in Parliament), we were back in Stellenbosch. It was amazing to be able to listen to ANC speakers such as Albie Sachs and Thabo Mbeki on the campus, along with thousands of students. Only this time with a baby on my back. Not to mention going to the Student church to hear Beyers Naudé preaching, and to listen to the "Kraaie" men's choir from Wilgenhof singing "Nkosi sikelel'iAfrika" in his honour in Afrikaans. And to hear a farmboy stand up during question time after the service and say: "Oom Bey, I grew up on a farm in the Free State. I was taught that you were a communist. Today I want to tell you: You are my hero!"

But this apparent wind of change was deceptive, at least here in Stellenbosch. At the same time some of the "left-wing" students on campus started a campaign to have the name of Apartheid leaders removed from buildings, in order to make students from other population groups feel more at home. The names included DF Malan, BJ Vorster and HF Verwoerd ...

Their attempts were scuttled, however, by the apathy shown by most of the students (and lecturers) – by their insensitivity to the painful symbolism of these names. In spite of everything that had happened to me abroad, I didn't want to lend my support to this campaign in writing at first. I asked if the students were really interested in my point of view, or did they only want to make use of my surname and family ties, regardless of the implications for me and my family? What would my father and mother (both also linked to the university) have to say? Should a lecturer, particularly a new one who still has to earn academic respect, get so involved in student politics?

In the meantime I continued giving lectures (moral and political philosophy ... theories of justice) on the 6th floor of the BJ Vorster Building. I was sitting on the fence "thinking things through" and "not doing anything in haste". I resisted the temptation to make a gesture such as joining the ANC and repressed the need to "do something tangible". I was ideal prey for that trap of guilt and powerlessness.

(Perhaps that's why, when we went to Betty's Bay for the occasional break, I literally couldn't look Uncle Hendrik in the eye. It's probably also why when I walked into "Blaas 'n Bietjie" I got the irresistible urge to tear paintings off the wall or cover a bust with blankets, so I could "relax" and not have to keep suppressing feelings of guilt [and powerlessness].)

After spending a great deal of time weighing up the pros and cons I eventually gave an interview, about a year later, for an Agenda programme marking the 25th anniversary of Dr Verwoerd's murder. I had one minute to sum up my attitude to his moral inheritance:

Basically the policy of separate development boils down to the fact that good intentions and high-sounding goals were used to justify immoral means. The injustices that sprang from this unholy alliance also desecrated the goals and intentions. As Camus said: the means sanctify (or desecrate) the goal.

This warning is terribly relevant for today, but the moral heritage of Dr Verwoerd to me also signifies that we Afrikaners in particular must admit that his policy was not purely a tactical, practical mistake but a moral transgression, that we also have dirt on our hands. This is why we have a responsibility, a moral obligation not to trek away to deserted wastelands, but to stay here and get our hands clean, in a shattered community.

This summary, which I had written down and memorised before the interview out of sheer nerves, was never used. The off-the-cuff statement that my and other Afrikaners' preoccupation with their own historical pain made them blind and insensitive to the pain of other South Africans, was a better "soundbite". (At that stage, I was rereading Elaine Scarry's book *The Body in Pain*, a fascinating study of the politics of pain, the basic theme of the doctorate in philosophy I had enrolled for in 1990.)

A few weeks after this attempt to see numbing pain as a cleansing responsibility, on 28 September 1991, a wish of mine came true and I got the opportunity to convey the contents of my letter to Mr Mandela in person. A short conversation with Madiba and the reactions of certain people to the conversation helped a great deal to transform my destructive feelings of guilt.

At first I was just one of the guests at a cocktail party for interested 'whities' from the Stellenbosch establishment. Like the others I received a short, but friendly, handshake. With all the noise he didn't hear when I introduced myself. I left it at that. Jannie Momberg[5], the host, fortunately came to my rescue, as he didn't want to let such an "historic opportunity" go by.

I can't remember how I expected Madiba to react. In any case, his first words caught me off guard: "How is your grandmother? When you see her again, if she

---

5 Former Afrikaner nationalist, later MP for the Democratic Party, became an independent when he joined the ANC in the early 1990s, currently ANC MP.

won't mind, would you please convey my best wishes to her ..." He had never received my letter. He listened attentively as I more or less repeated the contents, but his astounding lack of bitterness made him answer: "Don't worry about the past, let us work together for a better future ..." Coming from him, these words left a very deep impression: "As a Verwoerd you have a great advantage, when you speak, the people will listen."

Next day Dirk van Eeden, who had also been a guest at the cocktail party and was a good friend of my sister-in-law, paid a special visit to express his appreciation to me. He wanted to tell me how much my handshake with Mandela had meant to him as a young Afrikaner who was wrestling with his share in the past, and consequently also with his conservative family in the country. Mandela's open-heartedness and the unexpected, clear affirmation that being a Verwoerd was an advantage made me realise a few home truths. On the one hand I was doubtful of my true motives in taking a public stand, and afraid of being criticised for using my name to draw attention to myself. On the other hand I was afraid of losing my identity in the process, and of being used by the ANC and the media to the detriment of myself and my family ... Yet I was passing up a golden opportunity to turn "bad news" into "good news" (Elliot). It suddenly became clear to me that it would be less selfish to start talking than to keep quiet. If the surname Verwoerd, at least at this stage of history, was an advantage, if it might mean something to other people if used in a certain way, then I would just have to live with the dangers of abuse, by myself and others. Use and abuse are two sides of the same coin.

But it was easier said than done. Dirk's teacup had barely cooled before my mother also called, and not only to see her only grandchild. She had read in *Die Burger* what had happened the previous night. She was very upset and worried that I might really be planning to join the ANC. Our family is terribly precious to her and in view of my father's distress about what I'd said on TV recently, such a step might very well bring about a major rift. She literally begged me, with tears in her eyes, to express my convictions in some other way rather than within the ANC, for the sake of the family.

The "baffling contrast" between my mother's tears and Dirk's handshake made me allow a few more months to go by before I made a certain choice on that Saturday morning in May 1992, with the help of midwives such as Stuart Fowler and Anthony Appiah. And for a few months more we tried to keep it quiet, so that the family in particular would not find out. The completed entry form lay around for a few weeks before Melanie sent it, along with other forms, to the regional office. In the end, a few months later, I had to fill in another form before I was officially accepted as an ANC member. Sometimes I wanted to tear up the first form. At that stage no one but Melanie knew anything about it, after all. It was during this time that Codesa II failed and the low-point of the Boipatong massacre was reached. The die was cast, however.

On the evening of Sunday night, 23 August 1992 the worst fears of my mother (among others) were finally realised. *The Sunday Times* had interviewed Melanie in her capacity as a member of the ANC executive in Stellenbosch. One of her conditions was that we could look at the interview before publication. In the original version the impression was created that I was not a member of the ANC. Although I did not yet have the green, yellow and black membership card in my hand, we felt this was misleading. To cut a long story short, in the end the story was titled: "Verwoerds join the ANC".

To my father, there was a big difference between being sympathetic to the ANC and becoming a member of the ANC. During a difficult conversation after my meeting with Mr Mandela in 1991 we talked openly about the issue. He warned me that if I did in fact join, our relationship would never be the same. Despite this, I underestimated the depth of his feelings about my decision:

Stellenbosch
24/8/92

On a rainy Monday morning, before the start of a full week of classes and preparation, it's good to just have a quiet moment. Especially after last night's strained talk with Ma and Pa. A talk that left me with mixed feelings.

On the one hand this was because they find our decision (especially my decision) to join the ANC so unacceptable. I actually expected this, but I didn't think he'd go so far as to say we were unwelcome in his house, that he would disinherit me (until we reconsidered our decision).

The intensity of his reaction – Ma is actually far more concerned about the damage being done to relationships – made me very apprehensive about future conflict with family, friends, Afrikaners (and other products of the total onslaught and/or Apartheid community). Along with the surprising number of calls and the BBC interview things have caught me a bit off guard.

Although I understand that Pa is looking at the world in terms of a particular ideology, it still hurts when someone (particularly your father) says "you are a traitor to your own people". And yet: while I write, and even last night, the dominant emotion within me is one of sadness and understanding for his behaviour. What he said to me does not upset me as much as the grief and fear that he and my mother display.

Besides, it was a relief to be honest and bring the conflict out into the open. It's better than a situation in which people lead double lives in order to avoid conflict. When I did that I never really felt welcome and relaxed at their home, anyway.

A few months later I started actively participating in the ANC's election campaign. The first meeting was a particularly emotional one, and it received an amazing amount of press coverage. Not only was the Parow City Hall – where the Conservative Party usually held its meetings – a stronghold of the AWB and the constituency of Hernus Kriel (then minister of Law and Order), but the political temperature in the country had been raised by the politically motivated assassination of Chris Hani a few weeks earlier.

To my family this meant a phone that never stopped ringing. Either people were looking for me (many people didn't know the difference between Mr WJ Verwoerd and Professor WJ Verwoerd, and in any case our number wasn't in the phone book), or people were ringing up to sympathise with my parents over their child's shocking behaviour. The result was that both groups rubbed salt into my parents' wounds, increasingly as the election approached. This didn't improve the climate for reconciliation within my family. Yet things were quite different outside the family.

(Sometimes the cries of "Viva, Verwoerd!" almost made me thankful for my father's actions – perhaps they had emphasised just how right my choice was? On the other hand my "thankfulness" really made me feel a traitor towards my mother – pulled apart by her conflicting love for two Wilhelms! And yet sometimes I enjoyed the media attention too much, enjoying the sympathy I got for having a divided family. Did this feeling have anything to do with a subconscious need to be "punished" for my share in Apartheid? The apparent rejection by my father might be a way to handle deep-rooted, persistent feelings of guilt, a visible form of penance that I had to carry out to make me feel better because at last I had to sacrifice something in the struggle against Apartheid.)

The "baffling contrast" between the vision of Wilhelm senior and the experiences of Wilhelm junior outside the family, aggravated by the seesawing of the exhausting negotiation process, often made me and Melanie feel, to quote Charles Dickens: "It was the best of times, it was the worst of times ... it was the spring of hope, it was the winter of despair ..." (*A Tale of Two Cities*.) (I even gave a speech on this theme, on 1 September 1993, the first day of Spring, with a memorial candle for Amy Biehl on the table.) My diary reflected some of the conflicting emotions I felt:

24/10/93
Elephant Lodge, Eastern Transvaal
21h00

... and then I ended up almost sitting next to Walter Sisulu on the plane (coincidence?)

Another "baffling contrast", after yesterday's unpleasantness at the house: with father confirming that we were still most definitely unwelcome, much to Ma's consternation. Afterwards a conversation with my brother Dirk (visiting from the Transvaal) in which the so-called differences between white and black and between black "nations" featured prominently.

And just a couple of hours later sitting next to Walter Sisulu and hearing about how much the prisoners on Robben Island missed their children. How they were haunted for days by the sound of a warder's child crying in the night, how the worst part of their ordeal was not being able to see their own children – and to think some of my relatives say: "but we are so different from them"!

(And when I question him about Dr Verwoerd he says it's important to see Verwoerd as a politician within certain structures and organisations, and Apartheid as a chapter in a long story of segregation, that it is wrong to blame the Boers for everything. He makes me feel I'm too critical of my grandfather. Perhaps he's just being polite, but I find it so ironic!)

His warm handshake and affirmation of how important history is in terms of maintaining perspective on the difficult road ahead ... and then I drive through the Eastern Transvaal, and hear on Radio Pretoria that yet another elderly farmer has been murdered on his farm, and then I talk to business people, some of whom don't want to sleep in the same rondavel as a "kaffir", and who worry a lot about "affirmative action".

In terms of the contrast between my father's vision and my perspective, happily it seemed as if a "winter of despair" was giving way to a "spring of hope". While he, for understandable reasons, compared my "defection" to the ANC with the parable of the prodigal son, I was inclined not to take this as seriously as I once might have done. I had found the more I "gave away" of my birthright, the more I "betrayed" my position as grandson of Verwoerd, the more I got back and the freer I felt to be myself ... as a tree bending in the wind, as a pigment-poor afrika-ner, even as a Verwoerd.

In a certain sense this experience confirmed what Carel Boshoff junior said at a family gathering at Verwoerd's grave:

"In view of the great changes taking place, other perspectives are opening up to us: particularly those of us who belong to the third generation of this circle. For us, remembrance is second-hand and must come from books and stories; simple homage might seem like a misplaced nostalgia that will not allow us to find peace; we can only commemorate and thereby reclaim our inheritance. But this won't happen according to a formula, with rigid demands and expectations of what the result should be. This can only lead to estrangement.

"I am not asking permission for some or other youthful experiment, I am stating my considered opinion that in the future Hendrik Verwoerd will live on only insofar as we members of the younger generation critically reclaim him." (1994: 6)

Ironically enough it was members of the ANC who made it easier for me to live with the bewildering contrast between Hendrik the Architect and Hendrik my grandad: from Madiba with his sincere concern about the wife of the man who played such a major role in his suffering and that of his people, his concern about the name that was removed from 120 Plein Street ("his grandson is in the movement..."), Walter Sisulu's observations on the aeroplane, other comrades who said: "people don't want you to write off your family, or stop loving your grandfather – we just want an honest admission that he, among others, made some big mistakes ..."; Professor, comrade Lourens du Plessis[6], who said: "You should never feel ashamed of your grandfather."

It still isn't easy for me to page through the photobiography of Dr Verwoerd and look at a photo of a small group of people studying a plan, captioned: "Dr and Mrs Verwoerd and Mrs Botha, wife of the Minister of Community Development Mr PW Botha, scrutinise the map of the suburb of Triomf during a visit there in November 1965. To the right is Mr Koller, an architect in the department of Community Development." And to turn on the TV a few minutes later and watch emotional interviews with people who yearn with all their heart and soul to return to Sophiatown, the township that was gutted to make room for the new suburb of Triomf (Triumph)!

Despite these moments of inner turmoil, I felt a deep sense of inner completion once I had made the decision to join the ANC. The Sunday after my baptism of fire in Parow I went jogging above Paradyskloof, on the western side of Stellenbosch mountain. On previous jogs I had tried unsuccessfully to find the path that ran round to the northern side, above Coetzenberg, the mountain paths that I had traversed a thousand times as a schoolboy and university student, and used to know like the back of my hand.

This Sunday afternoon something was inspiring me – perhaps the intense feelings I'd felt after reading the reports in the Sunday paper, under the heading "Viva Verwoerd!" I came across a faint track, overgrown in places, up a steep slope, down a rocky incline, through a donga – and suddenly I was on a familiar old path ...

On the election trail during the next few months I often experienced this feeling again. It was as if my old self and my new self were shaking hands, as if a grandson could now sing along happily with Comrade Verwoerd ... As we visited dozens of small towns I felt as if my consciousness was being expanded, in between the "Vivas" and the explanations of the RDP. Because instead of driving through quickly on the way to some holiday destination or other, or visiting relatives or friends in a certain part of town, we drove right past white South Africa to the places where most of the population lived: the places and people (and prob-

---

6 Professor in Public Law at the University of Stellenbosch; adviser during the Kempton Park multiparty negotiations.

lems) made invisible by "Separate Development".

In the midst of great poverty I was immeasurably enriched by my contacts with so many people ... "Cockatiel" and Annie in Willowmore; Kobus in Komaggas; Karim in Laudium; Mewa in Verulam. Naturally, I was also somewhat disillusioned by certain comrades and by the deficiencies within the movement. But I also started to understand something about the impoverishment of Apartheid, of the meaning of the word "ubuntu" – that a person can only become whole through other people (definitely not only "my people"!).

I learned to live with the mixed blessing of being a Verwoerd in the ANC. On the one hand my picture of the Architect of Apartheid was sharpened. This critical distance helped me to understand, to remember why so many people regard Apartheid as a crime against humanity. On the other hand my closeness, my family ties, also made me realise the banality of evil (Arendt), the fact that (I believe) Apartheid (and "Separate Development") was also a human crime. I realised more and more that Apartheid was not just an inhuman exception in the history of our country, an aberration, but also an example of what ordinary people, like me, were capable of (see Kansteiner, 1993).

The "spiritual experience" of inner reintegration that Sunday morning on the paths of Stellenbosch mountain were unfortunately not the end of that story. When you come round a certain corner you look out over Uniepark, the suburb where my parents live. On the spur of the moment that Sunday afternoon I decided to run down to Uniepark, thinking it might help if I told them about my experiences, especially those that weren't featured in the newspaper reports ... When I got to the house I was pleased to see that the cars were outside, the back door was open and the front door wasn't locked. But nobody was there. It seems that "happy endings" don't happen as easily as we wish.

On the way home I thought about a terribly sad story that Doreen/Mpumi Hani, a Stellenbosch member of the ANC, had told me a little earlier. It was about an experience she had as a young girl when she was working as a childminder for white children in Stellenbosch. One morning she got to work and to her surprise the whole family was crying their eyes out. She asked the 7-year-old girl: "What's wrong, why are you all crying?" "Haven't you heard?" replied the little girl in amazement, "Dr Verwoerd has been murdered ... and now the kaffirs are going to be able to play with us .. and they will kill us!"

I wondered again where this little girl's fears came from, and how it would be possible to give her a new vision. I also marvelled at the baffling contrast with the story of a couple of toddlers who had been playing on our lawn a few days earlier.

Our daughter Wilmé (the eldest Verwoerd great-grandchild) was sitting playing with a couple of little friends when she suddenly shouted: "I'm Mandela!" After a moment's silence the neighbour's son responded: "No, I'm Mandela!", after which there was a heated debate with all four kids demanding to be Mandela. With the peace restored all four little Mandelas charged across the grass singing the old Voortrekker song: "Aanstap rooies, die pad is lank en swaar!" (Come on cattle, it is a long and difficult road!)

I couldn't think of anything better to tell the terrified little girl who'd cried her eyes out on the day Dr Verwoerd was assassinated. All that I would like to add at this stage is: "Viva Wilmé! Viva little friends!"

Chapter 5

From "my girlfriend and I" to "Melanie's husband"

"The personal is political!"
Feminist motto

... if the aspiration to completeness is expressed anywhere at all,
it may be in our own muddled daily lives –
as many women and men are now trying to express,
in their sometimes bewildered confrontation with particular choices:
a commitment to work,
to citizenship and social justice,
to the care and raising of children,
to the household,
to friendship and hospitality ...
As they do this they sometimes encounter painful conflicts ...
This life can feel overcrowded ... It is frequently hectic, breathless, lacking in grace and ease.
And yet women and men who try to lead such lives frequently discover that these many values support and illuminate one another when all are respected...
... it is in their daily choices, if anywhere, that men and women will succeed in constructing a new and fuller meaning for that venerable philosophical expression, "the complete human life".

Martha Nussbaum, Women's Lot.

Melanie isn't the type of woman I thought I'd end up marrying. In any case, not when I met her early in 1985. She was the only rose among 30 or so theological thorns in the class I tutored in philosophy as a postgraduate assistant. But, as a former leading "Soldier for Jesus" and a prospective DRC minister I wasn't too sure whether she was really the sort to make a good dominee's wife. I thought she wasn't quite pious and serious enough. She wasn't a biddable, "good girl" like my two previous steady girlfriends – she even asked me to kiss her, and after we'd only known each other a few months, before we were formally "going out' and while I wanted us to remain "just friends"! (And oh yes, my dream wife had to be a good athlete, while Melanie wouldn't even go jogging with me – her great love was ballet.)

Now we've been married for almost 10 years. It's been a long time since I was the older lecturer and she the MA student. Now I no longer dispense advice to "my girlfriend" far away in South Africa, as I did in 1986. Helping her decide whether to make herself eligible for election to her hostel's House Committee, or consoling her when she wasn't elected ... now she's saddled with the awesome responsibilities of an ANC member of Parliament. Now she goes off on study tours to foreign countries while I try to take care of our two young children. No wonder that nowadays when I introduce myself to people they no longer say: "Oh, are you related to Dr Hendrik Verwoerd?", or "Is the guy from Topsport on TV really your brother?" They are most likely to say: "Oh, are you Melanie's husband?"

Sometimes, just sometimes, I wonder whether I should not have married a "nice Afrikaans girl" who "knows her place in the house" (like my mother!). Then my daily life might not have been so muddled. And my private life would certainly have been less political. On the other hand, without Melanie to help me make up my mind I might never have joined the ANC. In that case I would definitely now be very far away from the ideal of "the complete human life" (Nussbaum). So I often say to myself: "Thank God I married Melanie!"

My first memories of her are of a slightly built, shortish, freckle-faced girl with long, light-brown hair and a very upright stride – which said "nobody will ever manage to knock me off these feet!". She also had a clear, confident voice which instructed those present to "Please come in, we would like to start the meeting now ..." It was 1984, and Melanie was the chairperson of the Bloemhof Girls' High School Christian Students Association. My girlfriend, Lizbé, and I had been asked to give a talk about what our Christianity meant to us.

My performance was clearly not very impressive. It was only about a year later that Melanie noticed me again. And it took the flagpole at my family's holiday home to make her do that. In August 1985 we were camping at the Disakloof campground at Betty's Bay with the church youth group. While driving down to the cafe I decided to quickly look in at the holiday house to make sure everything was alright. Melanie and a few campers were in the back of the bakkie. While I was checking the house for signs of damage caused by wind and/or "redistributors of wealth" she asked one of my friends: "What sort of people have a flagpole in the backyard of their holiday cottage?"

A week or so later my connection to that "sort of people" ensured that she knew exactly who it was who was asking her to accompany him to the annual Rag Ball in Cape Town. This is usually the highlight of the social calendar, particularly if you're a first-year student – even though your companion might be a bit of a "nerd" who "isn't very attractive", as she described me to her roommate at the time. My family's love for the country's flag made her think twice whether she should accept the invitation, though. (Despite this, the night after I asked her, she had a clear dream that we would get married one day.) "You must be very wary of the Verwoerds, they are terribly conservative people," her mother warned when she heard about my invitation. The next time we spoke on the phone I was instructed to tell her about my political convictions. "Left of the NP," I told her, apparently passing that test. The night in the Heerengracht Hotel was a success, even though I couldn't dance, in obedience to the DRC's ban on dancing. The fact that I hadn't told her about my membership of the Ruiterwag on the phone would, however, become a stumbling block in our budding friendship.

After a few months of being "just good friends", at the end of 1985, I received the Paul Roos Gymnasium's Rhodes Scholarship. This meant we faced a difficult choice. I was supposed to start reading for my degree at Oxford in October 1986. According to Rhodes' will, scholarship holders must be unmarried, at least for their first year of studies. Then there was also the NZAV bursary for research in the Netherlands from July to September 1986. We had to make a fairly quick decision about where our friendship was heading. The question was, in less than six months could we lay a solid enough foundation to survive a separation that would last many months? If not, the only, less painful option in the long run, was to break off our friendship before it went any further. After the Stellenbosch spring I was no longer so keen on Plato's ideas about being "just friends" after all.

To cut a long story short, I dillied and dallied and Melanie's patience soon ran out on me. "Wilhelm, you had better decide what you want tonight! Do you love me or not? Just make a decision now or I'll kick you in the backside!" The result was after curfew time at the women's hostel I continued to pass pies and chips through the window of my girlfriend's room on the first floor. Cooldrink was usually passed through the bars on the window of the prayer room on the ground floor. These bars didn't prevent us from building a solid foundation for the future, or deny us the privileges of a steady relationship.

Politics, as I understood the word then, did not play a significant part in our friendship at that stage. There was, however, one night when she asked why I had to go to a meeting on my own, and why I couldn't tell her where it was being held. I consoled myself that I hadn't broken my vow of secrecy by telling her only that I had been a member of the Ruiterwag since 1982. She was definitely not impressed with my insistence that it was mainly a cultural think tank for "enlightened" young Afrikaners (at least in Stellenbosch). Why all the secrecy, then? And especially: why are only men allowed to join? Her stepfather and mother had told her many stories about the Broederbond's "you scratch my back, I'll scratch yours" attitude, so what was the difference between the Broederbond and the Ruiterwag? She had so many questions. I argued that I'd also been uncomfortable with the secrecy and exclusivity of the Ruiterwag for some time, but that I'd chosen to try to change the organisation from within since it brought together a group of influential young people from the Afrikaans community. This cut no ice with Melanie. She was chagrined that I hadn't told her about my membership long before.

This hickcup in our relationship was fortunately not too serious. About a year later, in 1987, I did resign from the Ruiterwag. My "rebirths" in Holland were to thank, though Melanie's anger was also an important contributing factor.

At that stage I was still the senior partner in our relationship. I was still "my girlfriend's mentor" rather than "Melanie's husband". I was the one who smuggled Mandela's speeches out to her from Maurits Street via my letters, and related Steve Biko's shocking story to her. I was the political educator who encouraged Melanie from abroad to explore South Africa, to go on an ecumenical study tour and to get more socially involved, for example on the poverty-stricken Cape Flats. I was the lecturer who helped her with philosophy seminars and all sorts of theological questions. I was the guide who sent letters to my "soft, feminine feminist" telling her about the world of gays and lesbians, of homosexuality, homophilia and homophobia.

In Oxford she was, as far as the outside world was concerned, first the girlfriend, then the fiancée and later the wife of a Rhodes scholar. Eventually she was also the pregnant wife of Wilhelm (also known as William, Willem, Bill or Will), and shortly before our return in July 1990 the mother of Wilmé. And all the while she was trying to work on her MA thesis. (When she wasn't delivering copies of *Oxford Today* by bike to help keep the wolf from the door.)

In Stellenbosch in 1988, the first year of our marriage, she also kept the home fires burning so that I could get my MA thesis finished in time. (That's probably why her Honours in philosophy wasn't going so well.) That was also the year when I went to find out about "the rest of Africa" at first hand and as a result started to question my Afrikanership more deeply. While I was singing "Back to my roots ..." on the deck of the *Mtendere*, Melanie was sitting alone in our flat ...

From July 1990 I was once again, in practice the "head of the house", despite my commitment to non-sexism. In other words I was the breadwinner and Melanie mostly the one who bought the bread, sliced it and spread butter on it – and all the while looking after little Wilmé. At the same time she tried to finish her MA thesis, on the "God as Mother" debate in feminist theology. And in between it all she supervised the building of our new house, with Wilmé, (often covered with sand, cement or wet paint) on her hip. I was usually too busy philosophising to get my hands dirty. Within three months we were able to exchange the flat for a house in Paradyskloof. Then she got a job as a temporary assistant (naturally) along with several other women (of course), in the University library for the princely sum of R9 an hour. It was the paltry going rate for someone with five years' postgraduate study to their name, but it helped us sink a little slower further into the red every month. Later she did computer programming at Stellenbosch University's Bureau for Continued Education, at twice her previous salary. But she still found the work terribly frustrating and unsatisfying.

This type of work outside the home worsened the unequal division of the demanding, unpaid work within the home. When a decision had to be made who'd get up to see to a crying child at night, or stay home to look after a sick child in the day, my job usually gained preference. "But Melanie, I have an eight-o'clock lecture tomorrow," or "I have to finish that paper (on the relationship between racism and sexism)" or even "Just remember whose salary keeps us alive." This often made Melanie observe, with a wry smile: "I'd really love to meet a practising non-sexist male one day!"

Perhaps this all illustrates why after five years Melanie still hadn't completed her MA. This type of experience definitely made her resolve to get more involved in politics at the grass roots level, especially when it came to women's rights. This was a decision that radically changed our relationship, and certainly made it more equitable. And it was a choice that helped me a great deal finally to swim against the stream of the Afrikaans community and the Verwoerd family, and all it represented. It was a choice that forced me more and more to put my money where my mouth was as far as feminism was concerned, and to admit that "the personal is bloody political!" It was a decision that makes me wonder, often in deadly seriousness, what it means to be a non-sexist man, and particularly a feminist father, in practice.

But I'm getting ahead of myself. Now more about Melanie's role in one of the most important decisions I've ever made in my life.

Our marriage was destined to become "political" right from the start. Even before Wilmé and Wian appeared on the scene, I tended to be rather introverted and Melanie more extroverted. This was an explosive combination (my sisters-in-law tell me that a relationship between a "fish" and a "ram" is an instant recipe for conflict). And added to this were the differences in our family backgrounds: my deep-rooted, often unconscious experiences of my mother – a Smit from Sannieshof in the Western Transvaal – as a traditional home-maker, as someone who gave up her teaching career to bring up her four sons full-time. And Melanie's intimate relationship with her "working mother" (who is about 15 years younger than my mother), a friendship smelted in the furnace of a divorce when Melanie was just three years old.

It was not only my image of my mother, of motherhood (and as a result of justice within the family) that was tested by my marriage to Melanie. Even my deepest religious convictions were brought into question. My personal daily prayer to God as "Father" was politicised by her philosophical-theological studies.

I was already well aware of the limitations of human language to describe the mystery we call "God". I was well acquainted with Jörg Zink's words:
All the images we use to describe God come from our human existence. God sees us, so we talk about his eyes. He protects us, so we talk about his arms and his hands. He has the power, so we say He sits on a "throne". He is far away and inaccessible, and yet he is very close by, so we talk about a "heaven". In order to describe a mystery we must use symbols or images; as human beings we have no other way of understanding. These images are not "correct" in the way a set of minutes or a multiplication table are correct, but ... they express a truth. They show Him who is the Truth ... (1980: 13).

But Melanie made me go a little further. Her MA research alerted me to the (potentially dangerous) excess of "he's" and "hims" in my language about God. Her dedication as a mother made me start looking at God with new eyes as "Comforter", "Carer" "Mother hen", etc. Her practical experiences at the seminary in Stellenbosch, among other places, made me realise clearly that danger was not only limited to the domination of masculine **language**.

When it came to the language I use to talk about God, her studies helped me understand that there aren't necessarily problems with masculine images of God. I was, however, inclined to forget about the limitations of God as "Father", "Ruler", "King," etc. In this process I often, unconsciously broke the first commandment: "You shall have no other gods before me..." (Exodus 20: 3-6). By looking through Melanie's eyes at this well-known commandment I was reminded all over again that it doesn't just refer to visible idols such as Mammon, but also images of the mind, to idols in my theology and the language of my prayers.

Thanks to Melanie I had increasingly begun to realise that when masculine language is used too much to describe the mystery that is "God", the "godly" all too easily becomes masculine as well. When "the truth" is a "he" then the man's word mostly becomes law. When "he" sits on a "throne" in "heaven", then I'm the "head of my household" and it's not easy to get me off that throne. If I pray to a "king", then it's "natural" to me that men make better "rulers" in the community. When "he" has the power, then "God" can easily be co-opted into the service of patriarchy, and I am inclined to accept male domination of society rather uncritically.

So it happened that outside my home and my marriage to Melanie I also started to experience my religion as political. This type of insight helped me understand that my "struggle for Jesus" wasn't quite as apolitical and pure of heart as I initially believed. Melanie was, in other words, an important midwife in my growth to become a "tree in the wind". Whose hands, I might add, no longer shook as much as they used to.

Melanie also played a more direct role in my choice to become openly involved in liberation politics and so necessarily get my hands dirty. In this process a very special woman supported her.

We got to know Nomajoni Makoena as Emily. This was in May 1988 when as newlyweds we helped look after an older friend's home and children. Melanie and Emily – a young Xhosa-speaking woman from the Cradock district, with a one-year-old baby on her back – very soon "clicked". This type of friendship – Melanie's spontaneous emotional involvement with Emily's world, Emily's openheartedness and quiet self-assurance, was something new to me.

It is still something extraordinary – in the midst of all the complications that usually bedevil friendships across the lines of race and economic class barriers: the type of friendships that typically go with the worker/boss situation, particularly in South Africa. Emily ... Nomajoni ... was surely one of the people who did most to remove the blinkers from my eyes: the blinkers that made me drive nervously past faceless "blacks" and look past the daily struggle in Kaya Mandi with liberal ignorance. Nomajoni was, however, not just a midwife in the process of my rebirth as a "comrade".

Luckily Melanie and Emily remained in contact during our stay in England. In 1988 Emily had expressed the desire to help bring up our children one day. Early in 1991 she started to work for us and I can honestly say she rescued us from domestic chaos. Nomajoni prevented our daily lives from becoming too disordered, considering the painful conflicts we faced with family loyalties, the time-consuming demands of raising children, and our joint commitment to social justice.

Perhaps I am just rationalising about this, in order to make Nomajoni's historically laden position in our middle-class white existence a little easier to accept. But while I fretted right from the start about the relationship between theory and practice in this regard, Melanie actually tried to do something about it.

Her viewpoint was that one should emphasise the quality and human dignity of Emily's working conditions instead of making yet another person unemployed. In 1991 she contacted the Domestic Workers' Union in Cape Town. Under their guidance she and Nomajoni started an agency that brought domestic workers and householders in contact with one another, subject to the guidelines of the relevant union. Perhaps I should say they tried to do this. Most of the white women who responded to the ad in the local newspaper were either shocked at the salary demanded – "How can you pay more than R200 a month for someone who gets food and board in any case?" or they found the whole idea of regarding "the servant" as an employee with rights (and duties) completely strange. Some of them just slammed the phone down in disgust when they heard the word "union". What upset Melanie the most was the fact that we knew some of these women, that the politics of peoples' private lives often differed so much from the public image of an "enlightened" Stellenbosch.

It was during this period, at the end of September 1991, that we met President Mandela. Shortly afterwards Melanie arrived home one day, after yet another distressing visit to an "outside room" where one of Emily's friends was supposed to move to: "Do you know, Wilhelm, when I drive along on these errands and see the houseworkers walking home from Dalsig and Die Boord to Kaya Mandi ... I've decided I'm sick and tired of that 'them and us' feeling. I really want to join the ANC ..."

As usual she was as good as her word. I supported her in this decision, but I didn't follow her example. At first we divided our labour: while she got her hands dirty as a member of a political organisation, I sat on the fence, for the sake of my family as much as anything.

Her exposure to often inhuman working conditions in people's houses, usually concealed behind high walls and worsened by the surplus of cheap, desperate work-seekers, led to our ultimate disillusionment with the "comfortable compassion" of white, middle-class "liberal" politics. The way the madams abused their power and the fact that the maids had no power inspired Melanie to fight alongside the people, alongside Nomajoni, for more justice – in public and in our private lives ...

After a few months Melanie was elected to the executive of the local ANC branch and attended weekly meetings with people from Kaya Mandi, Cloetesville and Idas Valley. Gradually some of those faceless people I'd passed on the road acquired names. Some of the women who trudged those dusty paths were now our "comrades."

Melanie had never been a member of the Voortrekkers – her mother didn't have the time to drive the kids round to Friday afternoon activities, and besides as an individualist she was uncomfortable with activities related to the "volk". Nonetheless her reconnaissance work was highly successful in helping this former ace tracker to find his way to the ANC. Her example encouraged me to make peace with my family's inextricable entanglement with the painful national politics of the last few decades. It made me decide not to allow that part of my personal life to prevent me from indulging in a public political involvement any longer. Her sensitivity played an important role in my readiness to stop dilly-dallying and be a little more daring and, by so doing, to unlock the positive potential of being a Verwoerd.

After years of friendship with someone who lived life so intensely, who trusted her instinct (sixth sense? right brain?) a lot more than I did when it came to people and difficult decisions, after hours of emotional conflict with Melanie, by May 1992 I was relatively in touch with my feelings. This helped me overcome my tendency to live too much in my head – thanks, among other things, to a male dominated family background, a "men don't cry" socialisation process and my philosophical training. It was this tendency that made John Carlin, a reporter for *The Independent* (London) quote from *Hamlet* after listening to the story of how I almost did not make the decision to join the ANC:

> *Thus conscience does make cowards of us all*
> *And thus the native hue of resolution*
> *Is sicklied o'er with the pale cast of thought*
> *And enterprises of great pith and moment*
> *With this regard their currents turn awry*
> *And lose the name of action ...*

Thanks in large part to my friendship with a more sensitive Melanie the "native hue of resolution" that had been conjured up by Appiah's book in May 1992 could lead eventually to my decision and turned into an "enterprise of great pith and moment". When it really came to the "crunch of decision-making" (Lucas), I could depend on my gut feeling, even though all sorts of questions still plagued me. As I was later to answer a common question: "I joined the ANC because I felt it was the right thing to do and this feeling wouldn't go away."

My exposure to the mass media really came a few months after my private decision to fill in an ANC membership form – once again, in a certain sense, thanks to Melanie. In August 1992 "Oom Angel", in a cynical report on the back page of *Die Suid-Afrikaan*, referred to "a rose by any other name". He had heard somewhere that a certain Melanie Verwoerd was now an ANC member in Stellenbosch. He wondered if this was a way of "cleansing" a certain family name. The report was followed up by two lines in *The Argus* the following day, which in turn attracted the attention of a reporter on the *Sunday Times*. At first Melanie didn't want to respond to his request, because at that stage we still hadn't told my family that both of us were members of the ANC. Melanie was basically offered the following option: either she co-operate and get a chance to put her side of the story, or the reporter would use other, probably less well disposed sources. In the end he asked my parents for comment ... this really set the cat among the pigeons and my father's distressed reaction was by now old news.

From that Sunday on we were not only unwelcome in my parents' house, but we had to learn to handle the unwelcome attentions of the international media at home. Melanie had to wait a long time before she received any recognition, though. She worked very hard in the ANC, and was even chosen to the executive of the Western Cape Regional executive, but the public was apparently not interested in the political activities of the wife of "the real Verwoerd".

This was not just a time of conflict within and outside the family. As the election campaign built up steam the conflict with my father, and our struggle to keep so many balls in the air at once, seemed to intensify. But through the bad times there was always a moment to toyi-toyi, to yell out Viva! and to have a laugh – often accompanied by a tear. It was the worst of times, it was the best of times, as Dickens said. I scribbled down one of these lighter moments on paper, and perhaps now is the time to tell the story again.

A strange face at "Mooi Uitsig"

It was a hot Sunday afternoon, but the community hall was packed with people – older ones with jackets and ties, and here and there a dignified old fellow with a hat on. Women had babies on their laps, the young people wore T-shirts with a certain friendly grey-haired man on the front: the ANC was having a meeting in Gharies, because THE election was just around the corner. Most people proudly donned the badges and waved the placards proclaiming "the people's choice", which had been handed out along with the green, yellow and black flags at the door. Others were just curious, it seemed to me. They had come to see what sort of performance a Verwoerd would give at a meeting like this. (And this Verwoerd even had the first Verwoerd great-grandchild in tow. My wife was also with the campaign and I had brought our three-and-a-half year old daughter, Wilmé, along on a campaigning visit to Komaggas, Matjieskloof, Hondeklipbaai and other famous places.)

Instead of checking out the wildflowers in Namaqualand, as we had done on previous visits, we were talking about serious matters today. And of course we were some way away from the "white" town, on a hill that looked out over the place where everyone more or less lived together, until the early 1970s. After 20 years of "separate development" I had to drive 2 km downhill to buy an ice-cream and cooldrink for Wilmé – and that wasn't only because it was a Sunday. On the way back to the recently completed hall my eye fell on a granite name plate, surrounded by dusty plants and washed-out flowers, at the entrance to the "coloured" section of Gharies: It read "Mooi Uitsig" (Beautiful View). I couldn't help wondering whether Mr Koller, the architect in the Department of Community Development who designed Triomf on the ruins of Sophiatown, might have had a relative or two here in the Northern Cape.

In any event, the ice-cream and cooldrink didn't last long. After the prayer, inspired by one of the comrade's enthusiastic welcoming address, which included an emotional quote from Martin Luther King's "I have a dream" speech, I began to hold forth on the tragic ironies of "separate development". Suddenly I heard a desperate little voice whisper: "Daddy, I want to pee!"

My speech came to an abrupt halt as I excused myself to take her off to do the necessary.

"Now, where was I? The first, most important reason why I am voting for the ANC concerns the past: the great difference between the NP's Apartheid history and the ANC's decades-long struggle for liberation. The second reason has to do with principles: the principles of non-racism and non-sexism ..."

"Daddy, I want to go and listen to my songs. Daddy, daddy, DADDY!"

The car stood outside the door of the hall, but she wasn't keen to walk there all alone. And she wasn't in the mood to be pacified, as she was feeling a bit rough after the long trip by dirt road from Komaggas to Hondeklipbaai. Not to mention the ice-cream and Coke. I wanted to avoid a tearful outburst at all costs, so I led her to the car to listen to her music.

The couple of hundred metres to the car felt like an eternity – she hates to be rushed – watched by the patient, smiling crowd who were hanging in there to hear the rest of my speech.

Question time. An old man stood up and I listened with a lump in my throat as he described his experience of "separate development", of dehumanising Apartheid.

"Daddy, the tape has finished. I want to listen to my stories now..."

"Please Wilmé, please listen to the other side first. We are almost finished and then we can go home... come on now, you know what buttons to push."

But I was on the platform a little longer than I'd anticipated. I hoped that my little talk to Wilmé would keep her happy for a while longer. In any case, I'd asked some of the women standing outside to help her turn the tapes over herself.

But then disaster struck. After picking my way through a minefield of difficult questions and doing my best to answer them I got that sinking feeling again when I felt a little hand tugging at my trousers.

"Daddy, I peed all by myself!"

"That's nice, Wilmé, very nice. Now come and sit here with daddy. Please. Now, as far as the violence is concerned there are a few things..."

The audience listened attentively. Suddenly I heard a murmur and saw a sea of smiling faces. Wilmé had decided that the previous night's mosquito bites were bothering her too much, so she discarded her clothes and was now parading proudly around on the stage behind me in her new Little Mermaid panties.

Luckily the meeting was over, but it was still a good few hours' drive back to Stellenbosch. After all the handshakes and many friendly thank-yous, after a quick wash and the promised picnic in (white) Gharies's caravan park, it was a relief to hit the road again – even with Carike Keuzenkamp's "My naam is Liewe Heksie" ringing in my ears.

I comforted myself with the thought that the meeting had provided me with an introduction to my second year Political Philosophy classes for the following

155

week – about Susan Moller Okin's book Justice, Gender and the Family. *And I also hoped that my efforts might yield a few votes for the ANC. At least I was reasonably certain that a few of the residents of Mooi Uitsig would vote with a smile when they thought back to the strange election meeting that Sunday afternoon.*

When I think about that meeting in Gharies today, it's a lot easier to laugh about it than it was that hot, sticky afternoon. I was grateful to Wilmé, and Wian for keeping my feet firmly on the ground during an election campaign in which I seemed to do little else but speak on stages and give interviews to journalists.

Now the election is a piece of history. The heady feeling I got from hearing "Viva, Verwoerd!" shouted many times has gone. Now I am trying to make sense of what is certainly the most difficult part of the story. I am trying to understand why, nowadays, I tend to think that there is a question mark – rather than an exclamation mark behind that "Viva, Verwoerd."

During the last couple of months of the campaign – after a baptism of fire with President Mandela in a packed Cape Town Civic Centre (at the end of September 1993), Melanie also started addressing more and more public meetings, besides all her duties as a local and regional member of the executive. We were also both nominated as ANC candidates for Parliament, but we decided jointly that only Melanie would make herself available. It was a difficult choice. In the end we decided that Melanie should do it, because of her personality and greater experience, and the chance it would give her to make a mark for herself outside the home. I was more reserved and in addition I felt there was academic work I should complete before becoming too immersed in politics. Once we had made a decision, though, we still had the worry of the effect it might have on the children. Family friends such as Graeme MacLean were very worried about what "politics" might do to our personal, family life. We decided we should be prepared to make sacrifices, and besides it was relatively easy for me (like many other career "women") to plan around Wilmé and Wian's needs. Of course, this decision meant being referred to by more and more people as "Melanie's husband!"

At first I used this label as a light-hearted "angle" to introduce the subject of the practical implications of non-sexism. But after a couple of years of living with the stresses of democratic government on our rather unusual marriage, my heart is no longer so light. Being the husband of a cog in the (shaky) wheel of the new

Parliament isn't always a bed of roses.

It still warms my heart when someone called Elvis phones up late at night from Kaya Mandi in search of Melanie, and tells me: "Remember, you are alone because your wife is working for the people!" But at the same time I'm often amazed at how easily I lose my temper when we are in fact together, and how different the letters I wrote to "my girlfriend" are from those that "Melanie's husband" writes nowadays.

Stellenbosch
11 May 1994 13h00

The day after the big party in Pretoria, two days after the great excitement of Melanie's swearing-in to the new parliament .. is this why I feel so flat today – "post-revolutionary depression" (PRD) instead of joy over the start of the RDP?

But why, then, do I have so many negative feelings towards Melanie? – "the best of times, the worst of times"? Tonight I'm really frightened by the intensity of these feelings, perhaps also because of the dream in which I chased Mandela and a few other "comrades" out of our house because she and I were having a fight.

It's the same old problem we've been facing for a while now: jealousy of the ANC, of all the other people (men?) who she spends so much time with and has so much energy for, while she's often so tired at home. Last night on the plane I had really hoped that we'd be able to have a chance to talk, particularly after my disturbing talk with a comrade who was wondering if there would be enough time for the "reconstruction" of his marriage after all the years of struggle. But she was too tired to talk. (Another disappointment.. another day that's gone by without expressing these suppressed and undiscussed feelings...)

This brings me to the question of "for a while now". It has seemed like an eternity, and it has produced some very negative feelings in me – jealousy, possessiveness, self-pity. These are feelings that I sometimes felt before towards the children, or because of them, but now they make me fearful for the future. Sometimes they make me feel like running away!

What is new is, of course, Melanie's political/professional career, which has coincided with a very demanding time in our country's history. This has intensified the complexity of conflict in a family with two children, as well as the divi-

sion of labour at home. If you add to that my own uneasy involvement in politics, the exhausting media, and all the usual obligations as lecturer, as well as the conflicts in the office and my family ...

... For a while now I've often wondered what effect her difficult, exciting journey through the "outside world" has had on her "inner world". On the one hand I am naturally very proud of her and filled with admiration at how well she's doing in politics. On the other hand I sometimes feel as if I don't know her any more: it's as if the endurance, persistence, wholeheartedness and extroversion that politics demands of you sometimes also produces a hardness which makes me want to withdraw into my introverted shell, and makes me cautious and unwilling to share my feelings.

... And then I get tears in my eyes when the two of us stand, with thousands of other people, waving at the warplanes that until recently represented a hated regime, but yesterday honoured the "people's choice"... "the spring of hope, the winter of despair".

My troubles as "Melanie's husband", described in the above letter, probably weren't only related to the demands of her new political position. Perhaps it is timely to remind myself that her becoming an MP represented "just" a part of the politics of our relationship. It was the tip of the iceberg, albeit a pretty huge tip! Our relationship had changed irrevocably – Melanie now had a professional career instead of her part-time jobs in the "old South Africa". Our marriage now had to accommodate a full-time politician – the vaguely defined duties of a "public servant", the endless meetings and sudden crises, the phone ringing, the phone ringing and the phone ringing ... All these things make me heartily endorse the sentiments of the person who said:

"The most political of all decisions is: who brings home the bacon, and who brings up the baby!"

As far back as the Maurits Street days I had experienced the truth of this statement, notably through Amor and Johan's stormy late-night discussions. When I read in my letters to Melanie of their spirited negotiations over whose turn it was to look after Stian, I can't help laughing at myself, even though the laughter is sometimes tinged with a bit of irony.

And then there was Rudolf and his friend Pieter, as well as Karen and Mandy (to a lesser extent), who exposed my homophobic, prissy little soul to "sexual politics". They taught me that it doesn't necessarily have to be a man or woman within (or even outside) a heterosexual marriage, who has to take the extremely difficult political decisions about babies and bacon!

I realised just how much it had meant to me to live under the same roof as Rudolf and Amor. The experience thoroughly shook up not only my personal, moral mindset, but also my political world-view. It seems to me that this destruction was necessary so that, together with Melanie, I could reconstruct my present outlook on life: in which the inner rooms and the outside rooms, the servant's room and the living room weren't so far apart any more, in which the private and the public, the personal and the political could not develop separately from one another.

I am, however, amazed and often upset to find how difficult it is to put these views into practice. My (male) ego is more fragile than I thought: too often he rebels at home. Sometimes I get jealous – even though I hadn't planned it that way and it's an irritation, like heartburn – because she now earns a lot more than I do, because she usually gets preference when it comes to deciding who drives the rusty old Golf and who gets the new Golf. Sometimes I feel powerless because my former trump card, "but-I'm-the-breadwinner", has boomeranged on me. Often "Melanie's husband" finds himself wrestling with all sorts of rebellious thoughts – especially when my mother shows concern over me, or asks why Wilmé is so pale or why Wian's nose is always running, or why Melanie is always having to go to Cape Town. Sometimes my ego hankers after the "good old days" when I was still basically cock of the walk – before Melanie and I made a few decisions.

There is, however, another side to the story, of course. I am often only too pleased not to be in her shoes. But because I love her I don't want to disengage myself from her demanding new (sometimes dirty) job.

Take, for example, a meeting we attended in Bredasdorp. The place was easy to find, because before the Election I had twice driven through the deserted "white" centre of town to the Windmeul, a (respectable) nightspot where the ANC was holding a meeting for free, because the owner's heart was in the right place. It was great to see old faces, and the hall was even festooned with old ANC election posters showing Mandela's face. As I recall, the slogans beneath the face, the "VOTE ANC!" and "FOR A BETTER LIFE FOR ALL!" had been cut off the posters.

This time the people weren't here to be told why they should vote for the ANC. It was a "People's Forum" just a few months after the Election, but the people – who lived in the local squatter camp and surrounding township – wanted to know what had become of the ANC's "better life" promises. For almost two hours I sat and listened to Melanie – the other speakers had not turned up – being buffeted by the winds of their frustrated expectations.

After the welcome – which did not include many Vivas – Melanie tried to briefly explain what the people's representatives in Parliament were doing. The empty benches in the main hall, which were often shown on the TV news, were deceptive. Most of her time is spent in other meetings. There are regular meetings of the standing committees and their sub-committees which have to approve legislation before it can be passed by the General Assembly. For example, she sits on the committee for Constitutional Affairs, and helped to co-ordinate a sub-committee responsible for the thorny legislation governing the process of transition to democratic Local Authorities.

In the past these committees did not play a very active, critical role in the legislative process. Like Parliament in general these committees were basically a rubber stamp for the legislative initiatives of Cabinet ministers (and their legal advisers). Judging by the complaints of NP members about all the extra study material, and the government officials' amazement over critical questions asked at "information" meetings, things are changing pretty radically. If people don't believe what Melanie says, for the first time they are also welcome to attend the proceedings of these committees!

While she was giving a short overview of the decline in political violence, the slow but steady progress that was being made in the planning of RDP projects, the introduction of certain free medical services, the feeding projects for certain schools, South Africa's re-admission to the international community ... I sat and thought about some other things MPs had to do that I had only recently become aware of.

The weekly ANC caucus meetings – again it seems that our comrades are not prepared to simply act as yes-men to the cabinet, or even the President, as MPs did in the past. There are also meetings of ANC representatives from the Western

Cape to discuss regional progammes ... As the sittings usually last until late at night, permission has to be requested to attend meetings in the "constituency" (which includes Stellenbosch, the Strand, Somerset West, Laingsburg, Touwsrivier and Worcester) with four or five other MPs. Then there are also meetings of branch executives, annual general meetings, meetings with local authorities, meetings of RDP forums, public meetings and "People's Forums". On weekends there are workshops to attend, and contact to be made with people outside Parliament (both within and outside the ANC) ... In between it all there are the people who never stop phoning or making appointments to discuss problems at work, the lack of work, houses with leaky roofs, etc., etc. And all of this has to be done without proper support services – one secretary between 20 or more MPs, no research assistants, no computers, etc., etc. Melanie has even hired someone to help full-time with all the office work and answering the phones, but she still can't get it all done ...

Her speech (and my thoughts) seemed to be very far removed from the people in this hall. The first few questions deepened my feelings of unease. The people basically wanted to know: "But what about us here in Bredasdorp?" The time to vote ANC was past – the time for joining forces to fight an election against a common enemy. Now the residents of the squatter camp wanted to know when something was going to be done about their problems. "Why are there only two taps for 700 people ... TWO taps for 700 people?" asked a female comrade (she stood up several more times to ask questions, whether it was her turn or not, but was somewhat mollified by a promise that we would go to the squatter camp after the meeting to see the problems first hand). "Why is there no work for black people here in Bredasdorp? ... only the coloureds get jobs ... the Boers tell us to 'go ask Mandela' ..." "Why can't we also get water and lights for nothing ... why isn't our debt also written off, like theirs?" were some of the other questions from the crowd.

Melanie tried to get some perspective on the question of "them" versus "us" which seemed to obsess the questioners, but the after effects of Apartheid were so well entrenched, the sharp teeth of "separate development" had lost none of their bite. The race-based inequalities between "the people" (particularly in the Western Cape) made me realise just how long and hard the road to a non-racial, democratic South Africa was going to be. She acknowledged the people's frustration with local authorities that still tried to live in the "old" South Africa, who tried to undermine the legitimacy of the new, democratic structures at national and provincial level and caused great headaches when it came to implementing the RDP. She emphasised that this was precisely why it was so important to begin work on the following year's local elections right away ... She was, however, interrupted by a grey-haired comrade: "Don't tell us about next year's election, that WE must work hard, that WE are all in a team, YOU must help us. We voted for Mandela! Don't tell us to be patient, we want help NOW! We are suffering NOW! NOW! NOW! NOW!"

How does one react to outbursts like this? How does one explain that the first General Election actually only solved one problem right away – that of the Apartheid state's crisis of legitimacy? Democracy in itself is not a solution, it is "just" a method... now we needed the right structures to start addressing the bread-and-butter problems together (and not even at a local level, at that stage).

What could I tell comrade Oscar, on the way to see the two taps for 700 people, when he asked: "Where is the old Golf? You really are driving a smart car now ..." Was I imagining it, or did his crooked smile actually mean "Is it nice being on the gravy train with Melanie?" Perhaps I was just oversensitive about the persistent criticism in the media, tired of people's snide remarks about "fat cats"... particularly coming from those who prayed every Sunday in Bredasdorp's big white church, asking for God's blessings on missions far away in "Africa" which were bringing the message of "streams of living water" (John 8) to "them".

Oscar's question still haunted me as I drove home. Why? Was it because I had felt that old familiar "traitor" feeling when I thought about Appiah's Africans; guilt about being "paid" (even though it was Melanie who was earning the money – more in a month than she'd previously earned in a year!) made me wonder anew about how honest my "African-ness" really was after all. Or was it the involuntary feelings of guilt when I listened to the old man's raw emotions – isn't there more that we could do? Was it the shocking contrast between the two taps and the soothing sound of classical music in my ears (coming out of four speakers)? How did this fit in to my long personal history of ethical and theological reflection on the ideal of a "simple lifestyle", my lecturing on theories of justice and equality? Not to mention the sense of powerlessness over the painfully slow turning of the wheels of state in comparison with the speedy progress of the "gravy train".

I had a lot of time to reflect on the Windmeul meeting on the way home, because Melanie was lying curled up on the back seat – she'd had a long, busy day in Parliament and a very stressful evening, and she was coming down with a migraine.

Was it "just" the stress, or was it also, on a deeper level, the jaws of Charles Elliot's trap having a field day? If I look deep inside myself I am inclined to answer "yes" to the second question. I often find myself trapped once again in the jaws of those feelings of guilt and powerlessness. I am also more certain every day that I wouldn't like to do Melanie's job, no matter how great the rewards. I worry about how she is going to handle the pace. I also worry about whether we'll be able to keep up the momentum of the current democratisation process in Parliament without more support services (and in our case, the democratisation of our household as well).

I find myself getting more and more annoyed by people – friends, relatives, comrades, "the man (and woman) in the street," even the writer of my early letters to "my girlfriend" – who can stand on the sidelines and criticise "politicians". The cynicism about "corrupt, parasitic" MPs is to some extent justified and quite understandable. The question is, what becomes of politics when this type of condemnation becomes a self-fulfilling prophecy? The question is no longer an abstract one that I deal with in classes on political ethics. It's a problem I now have to deal with hands-on. Suddenly my hands also feel dirty when I hear the same old hackneyed comments trotted out about politicians. After all, my wife is now one of "them".

And as for me? I am trying to be a good father to Wilmé and Wian, before, during and after doing my job. I am also learning, slowly but surely, how to be an MP's husband and a friend to Melanie. As the philosopher Martha Nussbaum predicted, this life often feels quite disordered and it's full of painful conflicts. But at the same time I also feel I've come closer to the ideal of a fulfilled, happy person ... thank God, I married Melanie.

Chapter 6

Conclusion: A Commitment to Continuing Conversions

It is now the beginning of 1997, almost four years after my first appearance on an ANC stage. I still see clearly the hundreds of excited, smiling faces, I hear the singing and the surprising shouts of "Viva Verwoerd!", I feel those unexpected tears welling up. Sometimes I wonder what it would be like to have another meeting in Parow today.

I know it will be more difficult than the one in May 1993, though outside the hall the police will probably have a much easier task. Parow is still far from becoming ANC territory, but the AWB has been remarkably quiet since the 1994 Election. There might well be quite a few (holier-than-thou) people protesting against abortion, or frustrated victims of crime crying for the re-introduction of the death penalty, not to mention PAGAD supporters. However, the main challenge will be inside the hall: more tension and less singing, by fewer people – especially paler ones.

Some visiting comrades from the Free State, joined by concerned local ANC supporters, might well, instead of singing freedom songs, hold up enlarged copies of the recent Zapiro cartoon depicting the former chair of the SABC board, Dr Ivy Matsepe-Casaburri, singing the new song "You MUST love me" and the old favourite "Don't cry for me Bloemfontina" to unimpressed comrades watching premier Lekota's statute being removed, as part of the show "YVY-TA"(produced by "top down productions")? (*Weekly Mail and Guardian*, Jan 31 to Feb. 6 1997.) We will certainly not be able to sing again "Wie het vir FW gesê, om in Boesak se pad te lê, STAMP DAAI BOUDE LAM..." (Who told FW (De Klerk) to obstruct (Alan) Boesak ...) – our former ANC chair in the Western Cape and main speaker that night in May 1993 is now facing charges of financial corruption in his defunct "Foundation for Justice and Peace". Teachers struggling with bigger classes and fewer resources in coloured and white areas, or those who took packages, will probably hold up posters saying "Bengu: 0/10!!" Cosatu members will like to know "what has become of the RDP" with the new "neo-liberalist" macro-economic framework apparently taking centre stage? Others are likely to complain about "Affirmative Action": "Under Apartheid we were not white enough, under the ANC we are not black enough"? Others would complain that they still don't know who their local MP is. And it will not only be the grey-haired "Oom" from Bredasdorp whose patience about lack of water, sanitation, employment and housing will be stretched very thin.

It would not be possible to address these complex issues and legitimate grievances in one meeting. Most time will have to be spent to discuss the trials and tribulations (and successes) of the RDP, the international constraints, the national and Western Cape contexts, the legacies of Apartheid within which we are operating, as well as ways to make political representatives more accountable within a system of proportional representation ...Once people have had the chance to voice their frustrations, to listen to some answers, the acceptance of responsibility for mistakes, mainly in terms of policy implementation and the acknowledgement that, yes, many heroes of the (negotiated) revolution are also revealing distressing flaws, I do hope there will be the space to stand back a little from these often overwhelmingly real bread and butter issues.

For in the midst (mist?) of the daily grind of democratic government I often have to remind myself that these are the "only" issues we are faced with! Of course, the alienation of citizens from the modern state, the "iron law of oligarchy" within political parties, scandals and corruption in government and continuing socio-economic injustices are nothing to be complacent about, but at least these are relatively "normal" problems in any democratic country. Yes, the new government can and should be criticised for the way in which they/we are building, but the **right** to try cannot be challenged (nor are there better alternatives). At last, thank God (and a few others), at last our political home is no longer being built on the sand and the suffering of "Separate Development"! It is so easy to forget how close we were to a bloodbath that night in Parow, in May 1993 (amongst other places).

While we are having another Parow meeting in February 1997, it will also be tempting to overlook the fact that much more than winning votes and fortifying the faithful, this time for the 1999 Election, is still at stake. Granted, the ANC is (slowly, painfully) transforming into a political party and winning votes is increasingly the name of the game. However, beyond the strengthening of a power base in the NP dominated Western Cape, beyond the desperate need to build many, many more brick and mortar houses all over the country and beyond the foundations of our democratic political home beckons Luthuli's vision:

*The task is not finished. South Africa is not yet a **home** for all her sons and daughters ... There remains before us the building of a new land, a home for men who are black, white, brown, from the ruins of the old narrow groups, a synthesis of the rich cultural strains which we have inherited. There remains to be achieved our integration with the rest of our continent. Somewhere ahead there beckons a civilisation, a culture, which will take its place in the parade of God's history beside other great human syntheses, Chinese, Egyptian, Jewish, European. It will not necessarily be all black; but it will be African.*

I see now more clearly that at the heart of my involvement with the African National Congress is a response to this vision, a search for this synthesis, a beginning of an answer to the question: what does it mean, for me, today, to be a son of (South) Africa?

Obviously there are other answers. For many the ANC road to an "African home" is clearly (still) too black. But the question remains. And if the ANC fails to embody Luthuli's vision, I fail to see how we and our sons and daughters will be able to LIVE, to be at home in (South) Africa.

Therefore, when I'm greeted by only a few white faces inside a Parow hall and when I think about the many "brown South Africans" who sadly seem to be more comfortable elsewhere in more familiar NP territory, I would concentrate, again, on the main theme of my speech that night 4 years ago:

Is it possible to be liberated from Apartheid, so deeply rooted in the hearts and minds of so many of us? Is it possible to find common ground between, for example, Voortrekker "kamerade" and, especially, ANC comrades, while so many South Africans continue to live in separated worlds?

My struggle over the last few years to help build a family life where both Melanie and I, our son AND our daughter, can feel at home (i.e. can live complete human lives) and my difficult experience of the lack of life in my father's house have made me less sure about whether and how one can get rid of the patriarchal, racist roots of Apartheid. This has made me even more aware of the powerful graffiti on a Berlin wall in 1993 (4 years after the fall of THE wall, and billions of German marks later!):

*Who will break down the wall in our heads? (*Time Magazine, *March 1993)*

In response to this haunting question I am tempted to refer to a few nuggets of wisdom Wilmé shared with us a while ago on the top of Table Mountain, for, as the old saying goes, the truth comes out of the mouths of babes and sucklings:

Shortly after the General Election in 1994 Melanie and I took our two children up the cable car to the top of Table Mountain. When we got to the top Wilmé's sharp four-year-old eyes fell on a piece of land in the middle of the sea. "What's that, Mummy?" she asked. "It's Robben Island," would have been the correct answer, but of course it wasn't the whole story. "Well, how should I say...it's a jail, but not a jail for bad people. It's the place where people like Mandela were locked up because they didn't agree with Apartheid," was Melanie's brave try.

Wilmé's spontaneous, outraged reaction to Melanie's reply was: *"But then they probably just didn't understand what he was trying to say!"* After she had thought about it for a while, and before Melanie or I could react, she continued: *"Perhaps they should have just tried to listen a bit harder."* I don't think anyone could have put it better than that. Perhaps I should just add the following qualification.

My experience as a "prodigal son" in the ANC made me realise the truth of Comrade "Cockatiel's" words. "Cockatiel" was a muscular, stocky comrade from Willowmore, who was no stranger to the inside of a police cell. During a conversation with a "pale" member of Willowmore's town council who couldn't decide whether or not to join the ANC "Cockatiel" exclaimed:

"If you stay up on the hill you'll never understand. If you join the people, then you'll understand!"

I realise, of course, that the issue of my reconciliation with certain people and the search for common ground can't be dealt with so succinctly. So many emotional landmines still lie strewn around the post-Apartheid interior world, and they cannot easily be defused. Given where I am coming from I am particularly aware that for many white, Afrikaner (male) South Africans the current changes are quite traumatic.

This experience has been captured by a well-known Afrikaans writer who recently stated: "We do not have a fatherland anymore!". I think this is the main reason why my own father seems to find it impossible to make peace with our deep political differences: admiration for his father is so interwoven with loyalty to an Afrikaner fatherland. To welcome a son who is an ANC member into his house would be a betrayal of his father(land). (And that love (loyalty?) is the one thing which no one can take away from him?) (Is this perhaps also why, for example, former president FW de Klerk finds it so difficult to show remorse for the past instead of just regret: when someone recently asked him why he can't go beyond the acknowledgement that Apartheid was a well-intended policy which tragically failed, his response was something like: "Do you expect me to say that my father was evil?") Fortunately my mother is a mother – there are more rooms in her heart, though she is having a hard time to keep her love for her husband and her son under the same roof.

My father's continuing demand that I must "repent" before we can reconcile reminds me of the humbling words of the community leader in Northern Ireland, whom we met in 1989:

"Each side has their own facts, selected to confirm their own point of view. Each side forgets that the real facts are the feelings of the other side ..."

I take this point, but what I sometimes find quite frightening is the apparent lack of feelings on my father's side when I try to explain, in writing, that for me to meet his condition would be to become silent again – a silence which would, again, rub salt into the wounds of those dehumanised by Apartheid. Sometimes I can just sit back with a deep sense of sadness, because in my father's face I recognise the other face of oupa Hendrik. I see the "man of granite", whose principles, in the end, were more important than people. Perhaps I am getting an opportunity to feel the heartbeat of Apartheid – "darkness masquerading as light"?

Often this makes me reflect on Richard Rohr's warning that in our spiritual journey it is so easy to confuse "sins" with "Sin". When I now look back at my activist days as a "Soldier for Jesus", or how as theological students we were not allowed to drink, dance or commit various other "sins", I see more clearly how blind and deaf we were to the cries for justice, for a humane home for all. And then I want to say, with comrade Prof. Lourens du Plessis, "Thank God, we've lost our fatherland"... because a fatherland demands dying, a fatherland sacrifices people (usually in the name of God). Now, with the ruins of the old narrow groups around us, we might have more space to commit ourselves to deal with the legacy of the real "Sin", to recover our individual and collective souls, to finish the task of building a home for all HER sons and daughters.

We **might** fill this space, because my own zigzag journey teaches me that disillusionment must be well digested to be nourishing. (More) truth might not lead us down the road to reconciliation, but to numbness and even personal disintegration or, in our public life, to the "privatisation" of our citizenship (as De Toqueville warned many years ago). That is why I would like to round off these chronicles about continuing conversions with a schema representing different phases in personal (and political) change, which I got from my colleague Prof. Willie Esterhuyse. The more I looked at this schema the more I recognised my own personal/political journey in it.

Attitudes in respect of change

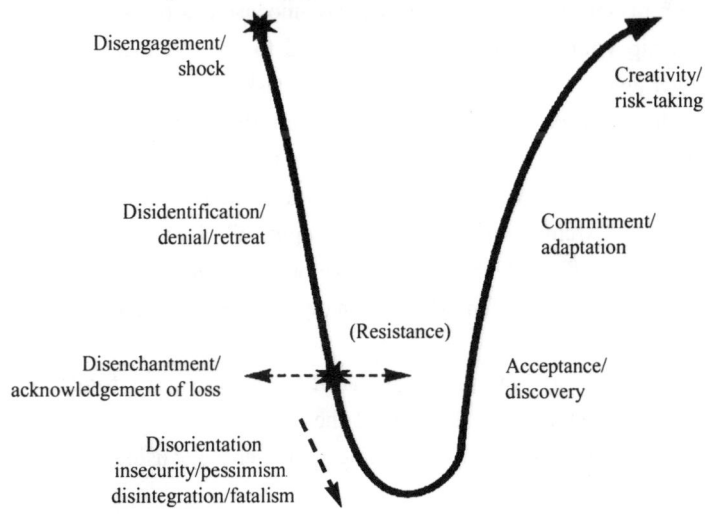

In the first place there was my shock, disillusionment and disengagement – from the DRC, from (white) South Africa, and from Afrikaners – that characterised the time I spent at 76 Maurits Street. Both Utrecht and my "first life" at Oxford were marked by a deep sense of loss of familiar certainties when it came to personal and political morality, often accompanied by feelings of insecurity, pessimism, depression – the feelings of being a ship without a rudder that I'd mentioned in my letters and diary. The tour "into Africa" in 1988 was the start of a phase of (re)discovery, followed by a greater acceptance of myself at Oxford, particularly through the research into my grandfather, South Africa and my history. This made it possible for me to achieve a new connectedness with South Africa and led to the decision to return, followed by the first two years back in Stellenbosch, where my Christian identity was refashioned. This paved the way to risk joining the ANC, and marked the start of the phase that I regard as one of the most creative, enriching and difficult of my life so far.

But in a certain sense the decision to become an ANC comrade was just the beginning of my road to change. With a few less patriarchal scales covering my eyes I now see how in my private family life more or less the same process of conversion was repeating itself. In a certain sense "Viva, Verwoerd!" is just a variation of the theme: "the personal is political". This time I'm amazed at the deep-rooted, patriarchal tendencies within me that I have to overcome, and at the intensity of the disorientation I often feel. But despite the difficulties, I am being forced to adjust, and to familiarise myself with new and previously unconscious parts of my self and my relationship with Melanie. I am challenged to commit myself to our friendship all over again, and to accept the liberating task of trying to make creative choices each and every day – of trying to "bring forth what is in you ..."

So what does it mean for me, today, to become a son of South Africa, given my early socialisation in the heyday of Apartheid (complicated a bit by being born into the family of the "Architect of Separate Development"), being baptised in a "whites only", "a-political" Stellenbosch Dutch Reformed Church, being systematically privileged by the colour of my skin, given my training in mainly European philosophy?

I think I have tried to say with this book that it means taking my forefathers seriously, dealing with the inescapable "sins of the fathers". It means facing my shame – it means standing up, opening up, owning up. It means not using the "sins" of, for example, the ANC as a smokescreen, hiding the "Sin" of remaining/becoming silent, of denying the need for the conversion of an Apartheid mind- and heart-set. It means a commitment to the need for continuing conversion while striving for as complete as possible a life for "all her sons and daughters".

I know it also means that there are no easy recipes for reconciliation. There are no ready-made plans and prefabricated walls to help build Luthuli's home. And, of course, this home, this synthesis beyond the ruins of the old narrow groups, can only be sustained if many more visible houses are built, if a creative redistribution of power takes place between those living in shacks and those with a house (and a holiday retreat), if ordinary people feel more safe in their own houses/shacks. I believe, however, that the truth remains: the cornerstone is a coming home to myself:

Even though "white" stands, rightly, for many wrongs,
Even though many white males are responsible for great injustices,
Even though white male Afrikaners and racism, sexism and tribalism are often closely linked,
Even though many white, male, Afrikaner Christians have justified these evils,
Even though a white, male Afrikaner with the initials H F and the surname Verwoerd has become, for most people, the personification of Grand Apartheid,
It is not wrong for ME to BE, amongst other things, a white, male, Afrikaner Christian;
I need not even be ashamed to carry the surname Verwoerd.
For the question is:
What am I doing with these sources of myself?
How do I transform being a Christian, white, male, Afrikaner Verwoerd from seductive reasons for destructive self-rejection to creative resources for reconstruction and true reconciliation?

Select Bibliography

2. From Soldier for Jesus to a Tree in the Wind

De Mello, A. 1992. *Awareness: the perils and opportunities of reality*, New York: Double Day.

Degenaar, J. 1980. 'The concept of violence', *Politikon*, 7(1), pp. 14-27.

Elliot, C. 1987. *Comfortable Compassion? Poverty, Power and the Church*, London: Hodder and Stoughton.

Fowler, S. 1993. 'Reconciliation in a heterogeneous society' in *Reconciliation in Africa*, IRS Study-pamphlet 306, Potchefstroom: IRS.

Rossouw, H.W. 1980. *Wetenskap, Interpretasie, Wysheid*. Seminare, Simposia en Lesings B7, Port Elizabeth: University of Port Elizabeth.

Zink, J. 1980. *Pad na die Gebed*, translated by L. van der Westhuijzen, Cape Town: Tafelberg.

3. From white Afrikaner to "pigmentpoor" "afrika-ner"

Appiah, K.A. 1992. *In my father's house: Africa in the Philosophy of Culture*. London: Methuen.

Chachage, C.S.L. 1988. British Rule and African Civilization in Tanganyika. *Journal of Historical Sociology*, 1(2).

De Klerk, W.A. 1976. *The puritans in Africa*. London: Penguin.

De Villiers, M. 1990. *White tribe dreaming*. London: Penguin.

Du Toit, J.D. 1944. 'Die godsdienstige grondslag van ons rassebeleid', *Inspan*, 4(3), pp. 7-17.

Harding, S. 1987. 'The Curious Coincidence of Feminine and African Moralities: Challenges for Feminist Theory' in *Women and Moral Theory*. (editors) Kittay, E.F., Meyers, D.T. Rowman & Littlefield.

Hepple, A. 1967. *Verwoerd*. London: Penguin.

Hountondji, P. 1983. *African Philosophy: Myth and Reality*. Bloomington: Indiana University Press.

Hugo, P. 1988. 'Towards darkness and death: racial demonology in South Africa', *Journal of Modern African Studies*, 26 (4).

July, R.W. 1968. *The Origins of Modern African Thought*. London: Faber and Faber.

Kinghorn, J. (ed.) 1986. *N.G. Kerk en Apartheid*. Johannesburg: MacMillin.

Kinghorn, J. 1990. *'n Tuiste vir Almal*, Stellenbosch: Centre for Contextual Hermeneutics.

Kinghorn, J., Lategan, B.C., Du Plessis, L.M. & De Villiers, D.E. 1987. *The option for an inclusive democracy*. Stellenbosch: Centre for Contextual Hermeneutics.

Malan, R. 1990. *My Traitor's Heart*, London: The Bodley Head.

Mithchison, N. 1973. *A Life for Africa: the story of Bram Fischer*. London: Merlin Press.

Moodie, T.D. 1975. *The rise of Afrikanerdom: power, apartheid and the Afrikaner civil religion*. Los Angeles: University of California Press.

Mudimbe, V.Y. 1988. *The Invention of Africa: Gnosis, Philosophy and the Order of Knowledge*. Indianapolis: Indiana Univ. Press.

Odendaal, A.A. 1990. 'Wit Afrikaan in 'n tuisland' in *Wit Afrikane?* Hofmeyr, M. a.o. Cape Town: Taurus.

Odera Oruka, H. 1990. *Trends in a Contemporary African Philosophy*. Shirikon Publishers, Nairobi, Kenya.

Praeg, L. 1992. *Die Self en die Ander: 'n Filosofiese studie van die self-definiëring van die Afrikaner in enkele geselekteerde tekste 1877-1948*. University of Stellenbosch: M.A. thesis.

Tempels, P. 1969. *Bantu Philosophy*. Paris: Presence Africaine.

Van Niekerk, A.S. 1992. *Sáám in Afrika*. Cape Town: Tafelberg.

Verwoerd, W.J.(III) 1989. 'A Personal Encounter with Africa', in *Into Africa: Afrikaners in Africa reflect on 'coming home'*, Stellenbosch: Centre for Contextual Hermeneutics.

Wiredu, K. 1980. *Philosophy and an African culture*. Cambridge: Cambridge Univ. Press.

4. From grandson to "prodigal son"

Ashforth, A. 1987. *On the "Native Question": a reading of the grand tradition of commissions of inquiry into the "Native Question" in the 20th century South Africa*. University of Oxford, unpublished D.Phil. thesis.

Boshoff, C.W.H.(IV) 1994. 'By die Helde-Akker, 5 September 1993' in *Verwoerd-Familie Nuusbrief*, 1, pp. 5-6.

Davenport, T.R.H. 1986. *South Africa: A modern history*. Johannesburg: Macmillan.

Elliot, C. 1985. *Praying the Kingdom: Towards a Political Spirituality*, London: Darton, Longman and Todd.

Kansteiner, W. 1994. 'From exception to exemplum: the new approach to Nazism and the 'final solution', *History and Theory*, 33(2), pp. 144-171.

Kenney, H. 1980. *Architect of Apartheid. H.F. Verwoerd – an appraisal*. Johannesburg: Jonathan Ball Publishers.

Lazar, J. 1987. *Conformity and conflict: Afrikaner Nationalist politics in South Africa, 1948-61*. University of Oxford, D.Phil.

Lucas, J.R. 1993. *Responsibility*. Oxford: Clarendon Press.

Luthuli, A. 1962. *Let My People Go*, Glasgow: Collins.

Morris, D.B. 1991. *The Culture of Pain*. Berkeley: University of California Press.

Paton, A. 1989. *Journey Continued*. Oxford: Oxford University Press.

Pelzer, A.N. (ed.) 1966. *Verwoerd speaks: speeches 1948-66*. Johannesburg: APB Publishers.

Posel, D. 1987. *Influx control and the construction of apartheid, 1948-1961*. University of Oxford, D.Phil.

Scarry, E. 1985. *The Body in Pain: the Making and Unmaking of the World*. Oxford: Oxford University Press.

Scholtz, G.D. 1974. *Dr. Hendrik Frensch Verwoerd: 1901-1966*. Johannesburg: Perskor.

Van Wyk Louw, N.P. 1981. *Versamelde Gedigte*. Cape Town: Tafelberg.

Van Wyk Louw, N.P. 1986. *Versamelde Prosa*, vol. 1. Cape Town: Tafelberg.

Verwoerd, S.A.J. 1965. *Wilhelm Johannes Verwoerd*. Johannesburg: President-Uitgewers.

5. From "my girlfriend and I" to "Melanie's husband"

Callahan, S. 1991. *Does gender make a difference in moral decision making?* Second opinion, 17(2).

Nussbaum, M. 1986. *'Women's Lot'*, New York Review of Books, January 30.

Okin S.M. 1989. *Justice, Gender and the Family.* New York: Basic Books.

Verwoerd, W.J. 1996. 'Tensions between my fatherhood and feminism', Agenda, 28.

Walzer, M. 1973. 'Political Action: the problem of dirty hands', *Philosophy and Public Affairs*, 2(2), pp. 160-180.

Acknowledgements

For permission to include copyright material in this book the author and publishers are grateful to: Oxford University Press for the extract from *Responsibility* by J.J. Lucas (Clarendon Press, 1993); Tafelberg publishers for the extract from *Pad na die Gebed* by J. Zink in an English translation by Les van der Westhuizen and for the extract from a poem by N.P. van Wyk Louw; Macmillan Ltd for the extract from *South Africa: A modern history* by T.R.H. Davenport (1986).

Every effort has been made to trace and acknowledge ownership of copyright. If any have been inadvertently overlooked, the publisher will be pleased to rectify any such omission in future editions.